Diy.
On a
Budget.

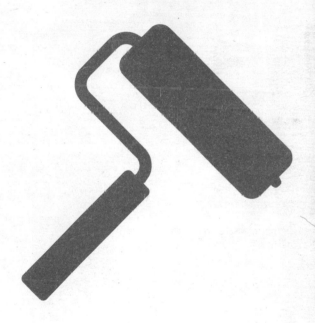

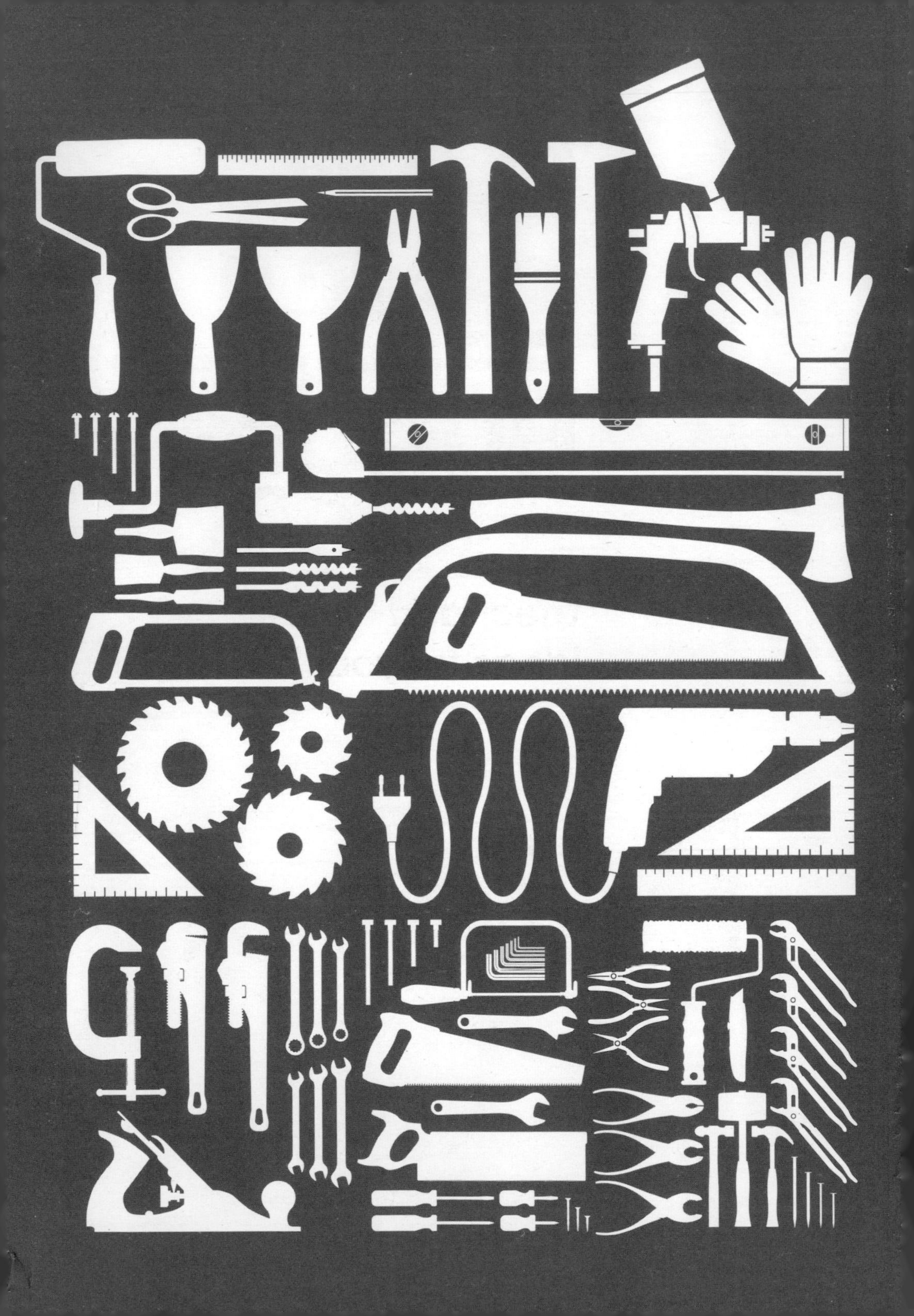

Diy.
On a
Budget.

The very best tried-and-tested ideas for your home

TONI
TREVILLION

BANTAM PRESS

TRANSWORLD PUBLISHERS
Penguin Random House, One Embassy Gardens,
8 Viaduct Gardens, London SW11 7BW
www.penguin.co.uk

Transworld is part of the Penguin Random House group of companies
whose addresses can be found at global.penguinrandomhouse.com

Penguin
Random House
UK

First published in Great Britain in 2022 by Bantam Press
an imprint of Transworld Publishers

Illustrations: © Shutterstock and May van Millingen/Illustration X
Design: Bobby Birchall, Bobby&Co

A CIP catalogue record for this book
is available from the British Library.

ISBN 9781787635586

Printed and bound in Great Britain by Clays Ltd, Elcograf S.p.A.

The authorized representative in the EEA is Penguin Random House Ireland,
Morrison Chambers, 32 Nassau Street, Dublin D02 YH68.

Penguin Random House is committed to a sustainable
future for our business, our readers and our planet. This book
is made from Forest Stewardship Council® certified paper.

MIX
Paper from
responsible sources
FSC® C018179

Contents

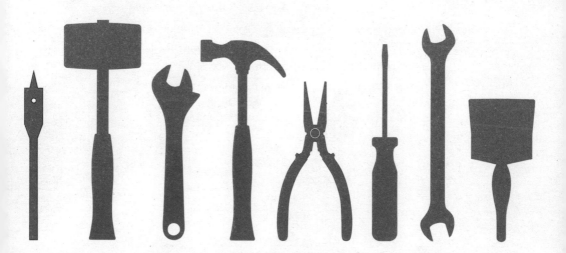

Introduction

Welcome to the DIY OAB handbook! Whether you're a DIY beginner or a bit of an expert, this book is bursting with tips and tricks to help you totally transform your home.

When I started the DIY OAB Facebook group, I had one simple goal: to prove that anyone can achieve a beautiful home on a budget. At the time, I was working as a cleaner on a zero-hours contract, and between feeding the kids and paying the bills, I didn't have the cash to hire tradespeople to help around the house. I decided that if I needed something done, I'd have to do it myself, and after a glass (or three) of wine, I tried my hand at wallpapering – my very first DIY project. Pretty soon I became a DIY addict, spending every spare second working on the house, sometimes making mistakes, but learning lots and saving even more.

As I continued my DIY journey, I began sharing my projects on the Facebook group, and to my surprise, other people started sharing theirs, too. A year later, I quit my job to focus on the group, and now, with the help of my brilliant community of DIYers, we have over 2 million members!

So here we are. I hope that in these pages you find not only inspiration but also a little bit of empowerment – as I always say, if I can do it, so can absolutely anyone! Good luck, and don't forget to let us know how you get on by sharing descriptions and pictures of your projects in the DIY OAB Facebook group.

Toni x

PS Thank you for making my dreams come true – you are all amazing!

7 Golden Rules for Budgeting

Before you dive in to your first project, you definitely need to read this section! Whatever you're planning, it's so important to consider your budget first. No matter how frugal you may be, it's way too easy to get carried away and end up spending extra cash that you could have saved. Everyone has their own budget tips (you'll find loads on the DIY OAB group), but these are my absolute non-negotiables:

1 **Set a budget and stick to it.** If you know what you're working with from the start, it's much easier to stay on track, and it'll encourage you to think smarter when it comes to paying for materials. Bear in mind that some elements of DIY projects can be expensive, but they're worth the investment in the long run, particularly items such as wallpaper and curtains that can last for years. Think of value for money when you're budgeting.

2 **Work with what you've got.** Don't splurge on expensive materials when you've probably got something perfectly usable at home. If you actually stop and think about the things you can reuse, you'll find you don't need half the items you thought you did.

3 **Do your research.** I live by the mantra that there's always a better deal to be had somewhere else. Never pay the first price you find – shop around, and make sure you check out online freebie sites, such as Freecycle.

4 **Go outside.** In an increasingly digital world, it's easy to forget that some of the very best deals can be found offline, in charity shops and at local markets, and so many items can be upcycled to suit your style.

5 **Use your network.** Before you splash out, ask friends and family what they have lying around. You'd be amazed what I've found in people's garden sheds!

6 **Use everything.** In my world, there's no such thing as an offcut. Absolutely anything can be reused. Whether it's broken tiles for a mosaic or leftover flooring pieces for a splashback, waste is a definite no-no.

7 **Invest wisely.** Spend a little extra on tools you'll use regularly. Take it from me, a paint brush you can use only once is not a money-saver!

Essential DIY Kit

Over the months and years, you'll find you end up accumulating all sorts of gear. If this is the start of your DIY journey, however, you may be wondering what basics you'll need to tackle your first projects. The following list doesn't contain everything you'll ever need for every job, and you won't necessarily need every item listed below, but it gives you a good idea of where to start.

- Tape measure – ideally a retractable metal one rather than a cloth one

- Paint brush and roller sets – these include a range of sizes to suit every task

- Painter's tape or masking tape – these are similar, but the former leaves clean lines and is less likely to remove existing paint as you pull it off the wall

- Protective kit including safety gloves, goggles and face mask

- Dust sheets, old bed sheets or old newspaper

- Claw hammer – equally handy to hammer in nails as to remove them

- Pliers – ideally a locking set

- Screwdriver set – with flat- and Phillips-head attachments

- Allen key set

- Adjustable spanner or wrench

- Utility knife

- Decorator's caulk and caulking gun

- Spirit level – these come in a range of sizes, get one to suit the task in hand

- Stud finder – you can either buy a physical one or download an app on your phone

- Power drill with a range of drill bits suitable for use on a variety of materials, such as masonry, wood and plasterboard

- Nail gun and assorted nails

- Sandpaper in a range of grits – fine (120), medium (80), coarse (40)

- Orbital sander

- Mitre saw – always use with protective kit

- Tool bag to store your tools neatly and be able to find them when you need them!

Common Mistakes

I've made more mistakes than I can count, and, I'll be honest, chances are you're going to make some too. Just as when you master any other skill, messing up is a key part of learning how to become a fab DIYer. That said, if I can save you from making some of the basic blunders I did when I was starting out, I will.

Below are a few of the most common slip-ups first-time DIYers make, and almost all of them are taken from my own personal experience. If you do end up going wrong, don't be discouraged! Try to see fixing each mistake as an opportunity to learn and build your skills.

Not cleaning your surfaces. If you don't wipe down an area before working on it (whether that's staining, painting, plastering or otherwise), you could end up with a lumpy finish, or even bits of fluff stuck to your wall! I recommend using sugar soap and a microfibre cloth, but if you don't have these, then warm, soapy water and a clean cloth will do. If you're working with wood, you'll need to sand your surfaces first, then clean them.

Using the wrong materials. It sounds obvious, but when I started out, I was forever choosing interior paint for outdoor jobs, or trying to glue down flooring with PVA adhesive! Always check you're using the right materials for the specific job you're doing.

Taking 'rough measurements'. Make sure you take accurate measurements, double check them, then write them down somewhere you won't lose them. There's nothing worse than beginning a project and realizing you're out by half a centimetre (or inch). If in doubt, measure again.

Using water-based paint to conceal stains. If you need to cover a stain, you need an oil-based primer or spray before continuing with your chosen colour, otherwise the stain will simply show through the new coat. However, if you're unsure of the nature of the stain, and think it could be damp or mould, then seek professional help to assess the stain as there's no point covering up something that needs to be fixed first.

Painting with rollers. To ensure you don't paint fluff onto your walls, prep new rollers by either rubbing them with your hands under running water, then letting them dry before use; or wrapping them in painter's tape, then pulling off the tape to remove any excess fluff. To reuse your roller tray without needing to wash it between painting sessions, slide it into a plastic bag, cut the bag to size and tie or tape it so that the bag fits the tray snugly. Whenever you've finished painting, simply remove the bag and throw it away. When you start painting, put more paint on the roller than you think you'll need to ensure you achieve a full finish.

Applying another coat of paint before the last one has fully dried. It can be really tempting to crack on with painting when the last coat feels 'almost dry', but doing this could result in having to remove both coats and starting again from scratch, so do ensure you leave enough time for each layer to dry. It will save you time – and effort – in the long run!

Not matching the batch numbers on your wallpaper rolls.
If you're using more than one roll, make sure all the ones
you buy have the same batch number, otherwise you risk
seeing a slight difference in colour between rolls.

Hanging your wallpaper pattern upside down. Again, this
might sound like a silly one, but you'd be surprised how
many posts we see about having to remove a strip that
has been pasted on the wrong way up!

Using lumpy wallpaper paste. This can result in real
problems – from the wallpaper not hanging correctly to
unsightly wrinkles – so make sure it's mixed properly and
has a smooth consistency.

Accounting for fixtures. Don't forget to account for and
then measure around fixtures and fittings that can't be
moved, such as plug sockets and light fittings, when
applying wallpaper or panelling.

Spot-testing. Always remember the importance of
spot-testing any solutions on less-visible areas of
fabrics – especially on much-loved items of clothing.

Substituting tools incorrectly. If a project calls for a
particular type of saw or drill, make sure you use that
tool, otherwise you could end up damaging either your
materials or the structure of your home. Remember, you
can always hire a piece of equipment if you don't think
you'll use it on a regular basis.

A lack of planning. There are times in life when it's best
to jump in head first, but DIY is not one of them! Do your

homework, plan the materials and tools you need, and try to work out exactly how much time your project will take to complete. It can be helpful to write down the different stages needed to achieve your final result: use the handy planners in this book at the end of each chapter.

Conversion Table

While this book isn't full of measurements, since you'll always need to take your own for your specific project, I make a few rule-of-thumb suggestions to keep in mind when doing certain projects. I've included these in centimetres (cm). For those of you who prefer to work in inches, many tape measures display both metric and imperial measurements, or there are online conversion tools. I've included a few rounded conversions below in case this is helpful.

Centimetres	Inches
5	2
10	4
20	8
30	12

Right, so we've got the kit, we've been through some common mistakes, budgeting rules and a conversion table.

Let's get on with some DIY!

Tips for the Whole House

Whether you're a DIY beginner or a dab hand, thissection of the book deals with a few basic techniques that are worth brushing up on before we start to talk about specific projects. We're including them here so you can refer back to them at any point.

We're also including some great tips to cut out some of the hard work, save time and help you stick to your budget while still producing an enviable new look for your home.

Paint

A DIY staple and one of the simplest ways to refresh your home on a budget is . . . paint. The power of paint should not be underestimated, as on its own it can transform a room or simply freshen up a tired-looking space. Here, we'll cover the basics of painting, including pretty much all the information you need to get started on your project, whether you're upcycling thrifted furniture, reviving your walls or making a statement with a feature wall.

> Picking the Right Paint

This part of the process is not only about browsing colour charts and painting swatches on walls, but also about considering where you are using it, what material you are using it on and how hardwearing you need it to be. So, consider:

What are you using it for? There are many types of paint – for indoor and outdoor surfaces, walls and ceilings, bathrooms and kitchens, wooden or metal furniture and accessories . . . The list goes on. If you're working on a specific project, do some quick research online to confirm the best paint for your job, but for everything else, the most popular DIY projects around the house are covered in the following list:

- Spray-paint primer and a primer for all multi-surface uses

- Interior walls and ceilings – typically use a water-based emulsion
- Bathroom – use an emulsion that's resistant to moisture and mould
- Kitchen – ideally, use a paint that's grease- and stainproof

'What finish would you like?' is a question that you may be asked when buying paint in store. The 'finish' or 'sheen' refers to the texture of the paint's surface when dry, as well as how much light reflects off it – matt gives a duller, more rustic look, while gloss appears shiny and bright. Your choice can change the way a colour looks once it's painted onto a surface, too, so consider the options carefully.

Colour psychology isn't a gimmick. Many paint professionals and interior design experts base their colour choice on what the room is going to be used for and the mood they want to create. For instance, in a social space such as a kitchen, you might want warm, uplifting and energizing tones, whereas in a bedroom you might want calm, neutral and peaceful shades. That said, don't let anyone or any rule deter you from a bright-orange bedroom if that's what you love – it's your home, after all!

White isn't just white. It's estimated that there are hundreds of shades of this popular neutral. Some are referred to as 'pure white' while others might contain a tint or undertone of another colour. Your shade of white will fall into one of two categories: warm white (yellow, pink or brown undertones) or cool white (blue, green or grey undertones).

Swatching and lighting. While considering different paint samples is important, it's also crucial to look at the swatches you've applied in different lights, particularly when it comes to walls and ceilings. Check each swatch throughout the day – at dawn, midday, dusk and at night with the lights on. Pay attention to how the colour changes and how it affects the feel of the room, as this will help you make a firm decision.

Tools. Your choice of tools will have an effect on the decorating process and the final result. They don't have to be expensive but they should be a decent quality. Look after them by making sure you clean them after each use. That way, they'll be ready and waiting when you start your next project, and they'll deliver a high-quality finish time and time again.

Toni's Top Tip

Always make sure to clean your brushes, rollers and other tools thoroughly. For water-based paints, soak your brush or roller in warm water for two hours, rinse until the water runs clear, shake over the sink and leave to dry or rub dry with a clean cloth. For oil-based paint, pour some solvent cleaner, for example methylated spirits, into a jar or a bowl, work the brush or roller around in it to dissolve the paint, then leave to soak for two hours. Rinse thoroughly with water, leave to dry or rub dry with a clean cloth.

Oil-based vs water-based paint

Before we get started with how-tos, let's spend a minute talking about oil-based versus water-based paints. As a general rule, most walls and ceilings are painted in water-based or emulsion paint, and woodwork is painted in oil-based gloss. You shouldn't mix paint types as water-based paint won't stick to oil-based paint, but if you need to cover gloss with emulsion, then sand the surface first to ensure your paint will adhere.

You don't need to use undercoat with water-based paint, especially if you're painting over a surface that is already covered in water-based paint. You should use an oil-based undercoat before applying an oil-based gloss.

When painting over gloss, you first need to sand the surface with fine-grit (120) sandpaper, then wipe it with a clean damp cloth to remove the dust and allow it to dry before you start painting. This is because any paint, but especially water-based, will struggle to stick to oil-based gloss and may even peel off in large patches once it's dry. A light sand and a clean will help your paint adhere and last longer.

Regardless of whether you're using oil-based or water-based paint, you always should clean the surfaces to be painted first, to ensure you remove all dust, grime and fluff before you start painting.

Water-based paint pros

- The surface you are painting doesn't require sanding first (except when painting over gloss)

- Less likely to allow mildew growth

- Low levels of toxic emissions and odours

- Spills and splashes can be removed with water

- Brushes and rollers can be easily cleaned with water

- Quick-drying

- Has a flexible finish that's resistant to cracking if the surface, such as plaster, expands or contracts

- Can be used on almost all surfaces (except unsanded gloss)

- Colour remains stable over time, and doesn't yellow or fade in sunlight

Water-based paint cons

- Colours don't tend to be as vivid or as rich as oil-based paints

- Not as long-wearing as oil- or urethane-based paint, and can be prone to chipping and scuffing. Can also peel off walls if damp

Oil-based paint pros

- Attractive gloss finish

- Good for high-moisture rooms (bathrooms or kitchens, for example) as water resistant

- Good for 'levelling' (where brush strokes fill in with paint to create a smooth finish)

- Hard, durable finish that's resistant to scuffs

Oil-based paint cons

- Gives off potentially harmful toxins and strong odours during application, requiring good ventilation

- Slow-drying, so you need to be careful until the painted area is at least touch-dry – this can take up to a couple of days

- Tends to fade or yellow over time

- Spills and splashes are harder to remove

- Brushes and rollers need to be cleaned with solvent cleaner

> **Preparing to Paint**

Whatever your paint job, and whether it's inside or outside, it's worth spending a little time to protect furnishings and fittings, flooring or patio paving from splattering or spills before you start. It saves a lot of cleaning up later.

1   If you're painting the walls or ceilings of a room, you might prefer to remove any large, special or expensive items of furniture or gadgets beforehand.

2   Lay dust sheets, old bed sheets or newspaper on the floor and tape them down. This stops them from moving about and makes them less of a trip hazard.

3   Cover all switches and sockets with masking tape or painter's tape to avoid painting over them.

4   If you aren't planning on painting your skirting boards, cover the top edges with masking or painter's tape too.

5   If you have old clothes that you don't mind getting ruined, pop those on. If not, you can buy disposable coveralls. Goggles can be useful if you're painting ceilings – to prevent any paint splashes from getting in your eyes!

6   Depending on the type of paint you're using and the kind of surface you're painting, complete your surface prep – including any necessary cleaning, sanding, removing of hooks, rawl plugs, nails or fixtures, and then filling in any holes or cracks.

Toni's Top Tips

To remove a stubborn rawl plug from the wall, use a corkscrew bottle opener – just twist it in and then twist back out again and the plug should come out easily. Don't pull or you might pull some of the wall with it!

To prime or not to prime? You should use primer when switching from a higher sheen to a lower sheen finish, like from semi-gloss to eggshell; if your walls have been repaired or patched; if you're painting a humid area susceptible to mildew, such as a bathroom; if you're painting unfinished, new wood or other porous surfaces; and when switching from a dark colour to a lighter one, or vice versa. When you're switching colours, tint your primer a colour that's similar to your final coat, to reduce the number of coats of paint you'll need to apply.

> How to Paint Like a Professional

There's no need to call in professional decorators at great expense if you've got a free weekend to do it yourself. Once you've painted one room, you'll wonder why you never did it before! To get the best finish, it's important to prepare the surfaces properly, and it's well worth spending time on this stage, as it will make the actual painting much easier and quicker.

ALLOW TIME FOR . . .

- **Preparing your surfaces**
- **Paint to dry between coats (see instructions on your paint tins for approximate timings)**

WHAT YOU NEED

- **Old clothes/coveralls**
- **Goggles**
- **Painter's tape**
- **Primer**
- **Paint**
- **Something to stir the paint with**
- **Paint brushes – ideally including a cutting-in brush for filling in corners, gaps and edges, and a small brush for touch-ups if necessary**
- **Roller tray and roller**

HOW TO

1   Pop on your coveralls and goggles – especially if you're sanding or painting the ceiling. Getting dust or paint in your eyes isn't very nice!

2   Make sure you have extra painter's tape near by, in case you spot any areas that you missed in your prep and might need covering.

3   If you're painting over a dark colour or onto a previously unpainted surface, apply a layer of primer first (see Toni's Top Tip on page 25).

4   Time to paint in your colour of choice. Stir the paint fully before you start, to make sure it is evenly mixed.

5   Start by cutting-in the corners of the walls, the ceiling edge and around any trim such as woodwork or fittings before you roll-paint the main surfaces. Cutting-in simply means painting those areas with a paint brush that you can't get to with a roller.

6   Now you're ready to roll. Pour some paint into your roller tray, then dip the roller in the tray and run it back and forth to get an even covering on the roller. You don't want a thick coating that is dripping but you do want to avoid painting layers that are too thin, or the end result will be patchy. Paint in a W shape over large spaces and make sure you go over the edges to avoid streaks.

7 Now for the least fun part of any DIY painting project – waiting for the paint to dry. Check the manufacturer's guidelines on the side of your paint tin for estimated drying times.

8 If your surface needs another coat, wait until the paint is fully dry before repeating steps 5 and 6. Two coats are generally recommended, but always check the guidelines on the tin.

9 Paint must be completely dry before completing the final step.

10 Carefully remove the painter's tape from your sockets, fittings and skirting boards, and touch up any little gaps with a small paint brush if you need to. Then pack away your dust sheets and clean your kit ready for next time!

Toni's Top Tip

If you haven't finished painting but need to stop for a few hours, you don't have to clean all your tools. Just pop a plastic bag over the roller or paint brush and tie tightly, or wrap them in cling film, to prevent the paint drying on them. They can stay like this for two days.

> Removing Paint Stains

Mistakes can happen, no matter how much prep you do – one wrong flick or drop of a paint brush and you've got a stain to deal with. Your immediate reaction might be to panic, but there's no need, as there are several easy ways to sort it out.

The best option is to deal with it as soon as it happens. If you didn't notice it at the time and the paint has now dried, you'll need to put a bit more effort into getting rid of it.

Here are three of the most common paint stains that happen during DIY projects, and how you can remove them.

Wood furniture

1   As soon as you notice the stain, try using something with a flat edge, such as an old loyalty card, to scrape up the wet paint. Note: if the paint is already dry, this won't work, so make your way directly to step 4.

2   Water-based paint stains should disappear just by scrubbing with a little water, soap and some elbow grease.

3   Oil-based paint stains can be removed by rubbing the surface with mineral spirits – this is safe for hardwood and linoleum. You can also use turpentine or acetone, but these can strip the colour of the wood, so always do a spot-test first on an area of the furniture that isn't visible.

4 If the paint has dried, very gently scrape or sand off as much of it as possible, taking care not to damage the wood beneath. Then you can use a paint stripper of your choice to remove what's left.

5 You can also heat up a dried oil-paint stain with a heat gun, then scrape off the melted paint, but again, do this very carefully, as you don't want to scorch the wood.

Carpet

1 If the paint is fresh and water-based, simply blot the stain with a wet paper towel – do not scrub at it, as you'll work it further into the carpet.

2 If the paint is dry and water-based, use hot water and a tiny amount of washing-up liquid. Mix the two together, then apply the solution to the carpet using a clean cloth. Leave it for five minutes to soften the paint, then use a blunt knife, old loyalty card or other flat-edged item to scrape at the stain. As you scrape, add more solution if necessary. To finish, rinse with a damp clean cloth.

3 If the stain is from oil-based paint, the most effective removal method is to apply steam directly to the stain, which is most easily done with a steam cleaner or garment steamer (or you could try using the steam function on an iron – just pop a clean cloth or rag over the stain and press down). As you steam, scrape the stain gently and carefully, and continue until it's removed, trying not to damage the carpet fibres in the process.

4   If the paint continues to stick, as a last resort you can try mixing a very small amount of acetone or turpentine into warm water and applying this to the stain with a cotton-wool bud. However, first check what type of carpet you have and do it sparingly and with great caution, otherwise you might damage your carpet permanently. Be aware that turpentine can wear away the backing of your carpet. If in doubt, test the solution on a corner of the carpet that's not visible, or on a spare bit of carpet (see Toni's Top Tip on page 58).

Clothing/Fabric

1   Scrape off as much wet or dried paint as possible with a spoon or a blunt knife.

2   Dip a clean cloth into some warm water, then blot (don't rub!) the stain.

3   Next, soak the stain with either laundry detergent or washing-up liquid and warm water, and repeat the blotting process.

4   If the stain is still visible, apply a stain remover and machine-wash the fabric – double check the care label beforehand so that you don't damage the item with the stain remover or the wash cycle.

5   Repeat steps 2 to 4 until the stain is removed.

Tiling

Tiles are an ever-popular choice in homes, and can be used in kitchens, bathrooms and utility rooms as stylish and hardwearing flooring, or to create an attractive and waterproof practical wall covering or design feature. They come in a huge variety of textures, colours and sizes, and there's so much choice it can be overwhelming, but they are well liked for a reason – once laid, they're durable, low maintenance and on trend.

Hiring someone to lay tiles for you can be expensive, but with a few tips and tricks there's no reason you can't easily do the job yourself and create a tiled splashback or a patterned hallway floor that looks great and doesn't break the bank.

Toni's Top Tip

Undertaking a tiling project can be time consuming, so you'll need to be patient and set aside a fair bit of time. You need to lay tiles carefully to get the arrangement right, but also, grout takes between 24–72 hours to dry and you always need to leave any finished tiling project a full 24 hours to allow the tiles to fully set. So, before you start, especially if you're thinking of laying floor tiles in your kitchen or bathroom, it's worth bearing in mind that they may become a no-go zone for a day or two! Follow my advice on page 34 to help you lay tiles but still be able to access these vital rooms.

> Picking the Right Tile

Decisions, decisions . . . Think about your budget, your personal style, the room's function – and, specifically, what purpose you want the tiling to fulfil.

Let's start with materials. The most common types of tile – ceramic and porcelain – are also the most cost-effective options. Porcelain is a better choice for bathrooms and high-moisture areas because it's water resistant. Glass tiles are popular, but aren't appropriate as a flooring choice as they can't withstand a lot of pressure from being constantly walked on or having heavy furniture placed on top – but they're perfect for splashbacks in kitchens or bathrooms as they're stain resistant and easy to wipe down. You'll find beautiful patterns and colours on cement tiles, although cement is a high-maintenance material that needs occasional sanding and resealing, and so is better laid over smaller areas.

The next thing to think about is the size of the tile, an important consideration because different sizes can either expand or shrink the look and feel of a room. In smaller spaces, larger tiles can make the room feel bigger, but smaller tiles can be easier to work with on bathroom or toilet floors, kitchen splashbacks, or around the bath or sink.

Once you've decided on the size of tile you want, the next step is deciding on the shape, which can be harder because there are so many options. There's subway – thin, glazed ceramic tiles like those found in the New York City subway system; plank – which have a wood effect; mosaic – a combination of sizes, colours, shapes and/or materials, set in a sheet for easy installation; and more. Each size and shape will create its own effect – subway tiles can add depth to a room while a mosaic arrangement can add texture and colour – so do your research first.

Five Alternative Tile Ideas

Here are a few ideas to liven up a bit of tiling:

1 Make a statement by placing two different-coloured tiles in one space; this works best with a neutral tile and a bright one to provide contrast.

2 Hexagonal tiles are usually used for walls but they can create a high-end look as bathroom flooring.

3 Combine different shapes to produce an unusual pattern – try subway tiles paired with herringbone tiles.

4 For something truly unique, check out mirrored tiles.

5 Non-repeating or geometric patterns can turn your walls or floor into a piece of art.

> <u>Preparation for Tiling</u>

Good preparation is key for a durable tiled surface. Ensuring the surface is smooth, clean and dry before you start will make it much easier to affix the tiles – and to make sure they stay in place!

Toni's Top Tip

Before you start tiling, plan the layout of your tiles to make sure they fit your intended space and that you have enough of them. Use an online calculator if you need help with your measurements. It's worth buying extra tiles to allow for breakages; if you don't open the packages you can always return them. Use your tape measure and a pencil to mark any tiles that might need cutting. Don't panic about buying an expensive tile cutter – you can hire these, or it's always worth asking friends and family if they have one you could borrow. Or you could try posting on your community's Facebook page – perhaps a friendly neighbour will be happy to lend you theirs.

> Laying Floor Tiles

Preparation, as ever, is really important when tiling a floor, not least because the surface has to be really hardwearing, given the amount of regular traffic it's likely to receive. When tiling a floor, bear in mind how much time it takes to fit the tiles into the space correctly and for the grout to dry and set. You must allow 24 hours after tiling a floor before you can walk on it. So, if you're tiling areas that you need to access frequently, for example your kitchen or your bathroom floor, plan the full layout, but do half the floor one day, the other half the next. Remember that floor tiles are heavy and thick, so you'll need a heavy-duty cutter.

ALLOW TIME FOR . . .

- **The adhesive and grouting to dry and set, following the manufacturer's instructions, as well as a full 24 hours after completing the job to allow the tiles to settle.**

Toni's Top Tip

Work out the amount of adhesive and grout you need based on the instructions on the packaging. Mix your tiling adhesive and grout in small batches, as you need them, to stop these drying out and to avoid wastage.

WHAT YOU NEED

- Knee pads/cushioning (you'll be kneeling on the floor for a long period of time)
- Chalk
- Tape measure
- Tiles
- Tiling adhesive
- Bucket for mixing adhesive and, separately, grout (unless you buy ready-mixed)
- Trowel
- Notched spreader
- Tile spacers
- Spirit level
- Clean damp cloth
- Safety goggles
- Protective gloves
- Heavy-duty tile cutter (these can be hired or borrowed)
- Tile file
- Grout
- Grout float
- Grout finisher
- Anti-mould sealant with a sealant gun and finishing tool
- Trim (optional)

HOW TO

1   Whether you're tiling a floor or a wall, it's best to start from the centre of the room and work towards the edges. Before you begin laying floor tiles, set them out on the floor in your preferred design. Use the chalk and tape measure to create markings for the placement of the individual tiles. Remove the tiles, stack them in small piles and put them to one side ready for use.

2   Prepare a small amount of adhesive following the manufacturer's instructions on the packaging.

3   Use your trowel to apply the tile adhesive to the floor in small, workable sections. Evenly distribute the adhesive with your notched spreader – use its wavy edge to form ridges that will help the tiles to stick.

4   Place your first tile firmly onto the adhesive and twist it very gently to ensure a firm bond. Repeat with all the tiles for that section, positioning the tile spacers against each flat edge between the tiles as you go to ensure they are all evenly spaced. Aim to carefully remove the spacers about twenty minutes after you've laid the tiles – this gives enough time for the adhesive to start to set, but not so much that the spacer gets stuck or that you dislodge the tiles.

5   Use your spirit level regularly to check the tiles are flat and level.

6   Use a clean damp cloth as soon as possible to wipe away any adhesive that gets onto the front of the tiles

as, once it dries, it's hard to remove and you could end up damaging the surface of the tiles trying to scrape it off.

7 If you have a gap between your final whole tile and the wall or a built-in unit you want your tiling to reach, you'll need to cut some tiles to fit the space. Don't forget to leave space for grouting – generally 3–5mm for floor tiles, to allow movement of the tiles. Measure the size of the tile you need, mark a line the required distance from the edge of the tile, then, using a tile cutter and wearing goggles and gloves, cut each tile with the top side facing upwards as this ensures the smoothest finished edge on the tile, with the least amount of chipping. Use your tile file if you need to smooth any rough edges.

Toni's Top Tip

Whether you're tackling floors, a splashback or an entire wall, you'll be using adhesive, grout and sealant. Work on the space section by section and your finished result will likely be neater, and there'll be less mess from the adhesive and grout. This is particularly useful advice when it comes to a floor-tiling project – even when you've started from the centre of the room as suggested above, you can still section the room, as you lay the tiles so that you can access the bathroom or kitchen when you need to, rather than having to stay away from these vital areas while you work!

8 Apply tile adhesive as per step 3 and place
    the tiles you have cut firmly in position on the floor.

9 You're almost there! Once your tiles are dry and set
    (follow the manufacturer's guidelines on the adhesive
    packaging for timings), it's time to remove the tile
    spacers and move on to grouting. When you buy
    your grout make sure it's suitable for the type of tile
    you're using and the room you're tiling – for example,
    waterproof grout is best for bathrooms and kitchens.

10 As ever, for the best possible finish you'll need to do
    some cleaning before you start. Remove all dust from
    the surface of the tiles.

11 Prepare a small amount of grout following the
    manufacturer's instructions on the packaging.

12 Use your trowel to scoop grout onto the joints, then
    use the grout float to work it into the gaps. To achieve
    a smooth finish, use a grout finisher and wipe any stray
    grout off the tiles using a damp cloth.

13 Once finished, don't walk on the floor until the grout
    has set. Check the guidelines on the grout packaging
    as drying times can vary.

14 Finally, you'll need to seal round the edges of the
    room where the tiles meet the wall or units. Do this
    by working from one side of the room to the other. To

ensure a uniform look, squeeze the sealant gun with the same pressure and speed as you go. See the Sealing Tiles box on page 46 for further instructions.

15 Leave for 24 hours to allow the tiles to settle before walking on them.

Toni's Top Tip

It's not as easy to lay out a wall-tile pattern as it is to do a floor one, but you can still prep this stage of the project to make it quicker and easier for you. If it's a simple pattern, use a pencil and a spirit level to mark on the wall where you want the top row of tiles to sit, then use a gauge rod or a length of wood with the size of the tiles marked on it to determine where all the other rows will go. Mark these points with a pencil too. Make sure there's enough room at the bottom of the wall for a decent-sized tile; if there isn't, you may need to move your pattern higher up the wall to allow for one. (There are plenty of videos online that will demonstrate how to use gauge rods to make sure your tiling is neat.)

> <u>Tiling Walls</u>

Tiling your wall follows many of the same principles as tiling your floor, with one advantage – you don't need to worry about not being able to walk on the surface while you're waiting for the tiles to set! However, this job still needs the same degree of attention to the preparation and finishing steps to ensure the tiles stay in place and look smart.

1   For the adhesive and tiles to stick well, you need a clean and even surface, so start by clearing the area of any screws, photo hooks, nails or other fittings.

2   Make sure you remove any loose plaster or old wallpaper, too – rub the surface lightly with some sandpaper if it doesn't come off easily.

3   Fill any large cracks or holes on the surface. Check that the area is level and smooth – you might need to do some sanding, especially over any areas you have filled, once the filler is dry.

4   Remove any dust with a quick vacuum, wipe it all clean with a damp cloth, and leave to dry.

These are basic preparation steps, so, depending on your surface, additional prep may be necessary – wooden surfaces require priming, for example, and raw brick may call for plastering first.

ALLOW TIME FOR . . .

- The adhesive and grouting to dry and set, following the manufacturer's instructions, as well as a full 24 hours after completing the job to allow the tiles to settle.

WHAT YOU NEED

- PVA adhesive
- Large paint brush
- Fine-grit (120) sandpaper
- Scraper
- Clean damp cloth
- Bucket for mixing adhesive and, separately, grout (unless you buy ready-mixed)
- Tiling adhesive
- Trowel
- Notched spreader
- Tiles
- Tile spacers
- Tape measure
- Pencil
- Protective gloves
- Safety goggles
- Tile cutter (these can be hired or borrowed)
- Tile file
- Grout
- Grout float
- Grout finisher

HOW TO

1   On plastered or plasterboard walls, apply a layer of PVA adhesive with a large paint brush to stop the plaster from absorbing the tile adhesive – do a first coat, leaving it to dry for 15 minutes, then apply a second coat, leaving it to dry overnight. Your plastered wall is now ready for tiling.

2   On walls that are already painted, give a light sanding; on walls that are freshly painted, lightly score with a scraper – in each case to give the adhesive something to stick to. Either way, wipe away any dust and debris using a clean cloth and a sugar soap solution and leave to dry. Your painted wall is now ready for tiling.

3   Prepare a small amount of adhesive, following the manufacturer's instructions on the packaging.

4   As with tiling floors, it's best to start tiling a wall from the centre and work outwards. This ensures that any cut tiles will be in the corners and can be symmetrical. Scoop up some tiling adhesive with your trowel and spread it across a small section of the wall – doing this means your adhesive won't start to set before you have time to position your tiles. Take your notched spreader and use its wavy edge to form ridges in the adhesive. Work horizontally and wipe off any runaway adhesive with a damp cloth.

5   Then start to place your tiles, using tile spacers between the flat edges of each one, pushing the tiles firmly onto the adhesive. Aim to carefully remove the spacers about twenty minutes after you've laid the tiles – this gives

enough time for the adhesive to start to set, but not so much that the spacer gets stuck or that you dislodge the tiles.

6 If you have any gaps between the last whole tile and the wall, a corner or a built-in unit, you'll need to cut some tiles to fit the space. Don't forget to leave space for grouting – 2–3mm for wall tiles is recommended. Measure the size of the tile you need, mark a line the required distance from the edge of the tile, then, using a tile cutter and wearing goggles and gloves, cut each tile with the top side facing upwards as this ensures a neatly finished edge on the tile, with the least amount of chipping. Use your tile file if you need to smooth any rough edges.

7 Allow the adhesive to dry, following the manufacturer's instructions.

8 Now you're ready to grout. Prepare your grout following the manufacturer's instructions. Starting in the centre of the wall, use your grout float to spread some grout across a small area of the wall, taking care to fill the gaps between the tiles. Do this step carefully but quickly, as the grout will begin to harden.

9 Wipe off any excess grout with a damp cloth then tidy up with a grout finisher.

Sealing Tiles

It's very important to seal around the edge of your tiling, especially if the area is near a sink or a bath, as water could get behind the tiles and cause them to fall off – disaster!

1   Take your sealant gun filled with anti-mould sealant and run a continuous line of sealant along the edge of the tiled area. Think slow, steady and even.

2   Use a sealant finishing tool or your clean finger to get rid of any lumps or mistakes.

3   Leave the sealant to dry fully, according to the instructions on the tube.

Toni's Top Tip

The guide above is for tiles laid in a linear pattern on a cornerless, flat surface. There are many other tile patterns to choose from – such as diamond, brick bond or herringbone. If you're tackling corners you'll need tiling trim, which is inexpensive but using it can be a tricky skill to perfect, so hop online to find easy-to-follow tutorials.

Fixing Messy Grouting

Messy grouting can be really frustrating. You've probably seen it and now you can't unsee it! You'll be glad to know that this common problem is a surprisingly easy fix. All you need is a toothbrush, a glass or jug filled with white vinegar, and a cloth dampened with warm water. Dip the toothbrush into the vinegar then scrub as hard as you can along the grout line, focusing on the messy sides. Wipe away any grout residue with the damp cloth.

Flooring

When many of us move into a new place or think about redecorating, our first thoughts go to painting, colour schemes, or perhaps furniture to spruce up the space, but what's under our feet often gets thought about last or not at all. However, changing the flooring can totally transform the look and feel of a room – taking it from old fashioned to contemporary, draughty to snug and warm, or just more practical and hardwearing for the day-to-day traffic that comes with family living.

Before you start ripping up carpet, though, or ordering new floorboards, there are a few factors to consider. How the flooring looks is important, but you also need to think about the type of room in which it will be laid, the foot traffic it will experience, your household set-up (do you have pets and children running through the space with mucky feet or crawling on it with even muckier hands?), the durability of the material you're using, how easy it is to clean and, of course, perhaps most importantly of all, cost. Flooring a large area can be pricey.

In this section we'll run through the vast array of flooring on offer, how to fit or install it, and, ultimately, how best to make the right decision when it comes to the type of flooring to suit your needs and budget.

Types of Flooring Explained

Some of this might be obvious, but knowing the difference between vinyl and laminate, for example, might just help you to decide what you want. Here's a rundown of every type of flooring you could possibly want to know about.

Wood

- **Solid wood** – this type of flooring is laid using boards made from a single length of wood that are fitted together using a tongue-and-groove system to prevent draughty gaps between them. The boards can be sanded back and stained any colour you choose, and as they're really durable, they're timeless in any home. The downside to solid-wood flooring is that it can be very costly and also has a tendency to amplify noise, so rugs are a must, especially if you live in a flat above other people.

- **Parquet** – these narrow wooden boards are fitted tightly together in a geometric pattern, such as herringbone. Again, they're really durable and long lasting, and can be sanded and re-stained to update them. However, because they're made of real wood, they can be very expensive, as well as a bit more fiddly to lay, depending on how complicated your chosen pattern is.

- **Bamboo** – an eco-friendly, sustainable-to-manufacture and inexpensive alternative to real wood, it can also be very durable. However, while bamboo will tolerate fluctuations in temperature and humidity, it isn't a waterproof material, so it isn't advisable to use it in areas that can get really wet, such as bathrooms, kitchens or utility rooms.

Laminate

- These fibreboard planks are covered with an effect such as wood, stone or tiles. They're really easy to install, are more durable than solid wood, very easy to clean and have the added benefit of looking smart without costing as much as stone or wood.

Vinyl

- This type of flooring comes in rolls or tile squares that are generally glued to the floor. Like laminate, it often mimics the appearance of other materials, such as wood or stone. Again, it's easy to install, maintain and clean, and is often very affordable, too. A much wider range of styles and colours is now available, which all look much more realistic than the old plasticky versions!

Tiles

- Again, a huge range is available, so what you choose will come down to where and how you want to use them, and your personal taste.

- **Ceramic and porcelain** – these hardwearing tiles are very similar in composition. Porcelain is more dense than ceramic, so absorbs less water. Easy to maintain, these tiles work perfectly in kitchens and bathrooms, although they can be a bit trickier to install because they're more difficult to cut neatly and fit (see page 36).

- **Stone** – durable and good looking, but that comes at a price, as they're a more expensive option!

- **Self-adhesive vinyl** – these peel-and-stick tiles are inexpensive and replicate the look of real tiles while being able to withstand a lot of traffic.

Carpet

- **Synthetic fibres** – this treated material comes in a wide variety of colours, patterns and piles. Classic and easy, but prone to damage from spillages and wear, depending on the durability of the material.

- **Natural fibres** – such as wool and sisal are long lasting and durable but can be very expensive.

- **High- or low-pile carpet?** Pile refers to the loops of fabric within carpet; low-pile has tight loops and shorter fibres, while high- or deep-pile carpets have longer fibres that are more loosely bound to create a softer texture. High-pile is a cosier, more luxurious option, while low-pile is harder-wearing, easier to keep clean, and better for allergy sufferers and high-traffic areas of the home.

> <u>Tips for Choosing Flooring</u>

So, now you're familiar with the options on offer, it's time to consider which ones are most suitable for the space you want to cover.

Ultimately, your choice will be dictated by the room in which the flooring will be laid, how it's going to be used and your budget. Here are some tips for picking the right flooring for your room:

<u>Which room?</u>

Think about the space in which the flooring will be laid. What is that room used for? Carpet is the natural fit for bedrooms, where people like to have something soft and warm underfoot, but you might prefer a harder surface, or perhaps a non-allergenic one. While carpet is a common choice for bedrooms and living rooms, different piles wear differently, and it's not the best idea to go for soft carpet in high-traffic areas such as hallways as it will go flat over time. Vinyl is easy to clean and maintain so is a natural choice for kitchens, as are tiles and laminate flooring, given how durable both are. Harder flooring upstairs might result in issues with noise, so bear this in mind.

<u>How big is the room?</u>

The larger the room, the more expensive it will be to lay flooring, so this has to be an important consideration when choosing your preferred material (see also **How much can you spend?**). Choosing a lighter colour for the floor will help smaller rooms to feel more spacious while darker colours can close in the space but can also add warmth.

What are the moisture levels like?

Bathrooms, kitchens, utility rooms and even hallways inevitably get wet, so bear this in mind if you're thinking of solid wood floors which can swell over time and need regular re-finishing. Vinyl and tiles can work perfectly here as they're water-repellent and easy to clean. Carpet is best avoided in high-moisture areas for hygiene reasons and also the inevitable water damage that will be caused over time.

How much can you spend?

Depending on the look you're going for and the size of the room, your flooring choice could be really affordable or cost an absolute fortune. You may have a vision in mind but is it realistic in terms of the price of materials and installation? If you want the wooden look, consider laminate as a more affordable alternative or vinyl tiles rather than porcelain. Consider too whether you're likely to be staying in your home for a long time; if you are, using a more expensive material that you love might be worth the investment, but if you know this isn't your forever home, your money might be better spent on a cheaper alternative.

Installation

You can, of course, save yourself money and fit the flooring yourself, as installation fees can be pricey and self-installation is perfectly doable. However, this is all dependent on how confident you are, your experience and the type of flooring you're fitting, as some options, such as large areas of tiles, can be much more complicated than others (see page 32).

Style

How do you want your room and the flooring to look? Carpets come in a variety of textures, colours and styles that can transform a room, while there are almost infinite laminate flooring options these days, with chic, grey-toned wood being a modern choice. Visit flooring shops, look at the DIY OAB group, search for ideas on Pinterest and anywhere in between. Don't be afraid to go bold, and remember that hard flooring can always be mixed up with a rug!

Continuity

Last but not least, think about how you want the whole house to look. Continuing the same flooring throughout the house, particularly on each floor and in open-plan areas, can make the space flow and feel larger.

> When to Change the Carpet

Quality carpet that is looked after properly can last for decades, but more realistically, in a heavy-traffic household, its lifespan is going to be between five and 15 years. Here are a few signs that your carpet has had its day and should be replaced.

Matting

One of the first signs of wear and tear is when the pile stays flattened down in the most frequently trodden areas. This is especially true for carpets made of polyester fibres. Once the pile begins to stick down, little can be done to revive it.

Stains

Whether it was an unfortunate dog-related accident or Friday night's takeaway turned into a disaster, stains can be hard to remove and even harder to hide. If you've tried everything (see page 30) and it's not budging, it might be time to replace the carpet.

Worn-out underlay

General wear and tear over time will reduce the performance of your carpet underlay, a layer of cushioning, such as sponge, foam or felt, that is laid underneath the carpet to increase comfort, add a degree of protection under the carpet and reduce wear. Once it's gone, there are few options other than replacement. If you notice an unusual feeling or sound underfoot in certain areas, it is likely the underlay has worn through.

Smell and condition

Carpets inevitably see their fair share of family life. It doesn't matter how much you clean them or if you even go over them with a carpet cleaner, they won't stay new-looking for ever. Eventually, you might start to notice a lingering musty smell, which is a sign they need replacing. It's worth noting that you should make sure the smell isn't the result of some other problem, such as damp or a leak.

> <u>Changing the Carpet</u>

Whether you've just moved in or simply fancy mixing up the look of your home, replacing carpet is a great way to give a room a lift. With so much variety on offer, it's a good idea to visit carpet suppliers to browse the different styles in the flesh and chat to advisers about durability and usage guides for the style you like – and, of course, cost.

If you haven't had a new carpet in a while or you're laying carpet over a solid floor, you might need to change or fit underlay, too. It varies in price considerably but can massively change the lifespan or wear of your carpet, so remember to factor it in.

Perhaps you've decided on a style of carpet but now you have to decide whether you want to save some money and brave fitting it yourself. Carpet fitters know the job like the back of their hand and will work quickly and efficiently (which is a bonus if you're having to clear a room and pile up the furniture in another room while the work is done), but installation does inevitably raise the price. It's perfectly possible to fit a new carpet on your own; however, we should advise this isn't an easy task and you could risk damaging the carpet or your room if it doesn't go to plan. So, make the decision carefully and, if you still fancy it, here are some handy tips for how to go out with the old and in with the new.

WHAT YOU NEED

- Tape measure
- Pencil and notepad
- Underlay
- Carpet
- Gripper strips
- Orbital sander with coarse-grit (40) sandpaper to prep wooden floors
- Wood filler
- Nail gun or staple gun if fitting carpet onto wooden floors
- Self-levelling floor screed if fitting carpet onto concrete floors
- Suitable adhesive if fitting carpet onto concrete floors
- Knee pads
- Carpet-fitting kit
- Pliers
- Claw hammer
- Utility knife
- Protective gloves, mask and goggles
- Vacuum cleaner

Buy a carpet-fitting kit. This normally includes a stretcher, a tucker, and a trimming knife or scissors, all of which you will need to install your own carpet.

Work out how much carpet you need. Measure the area and write down all measurements, including any smaller, oddly shaped areas, such as window bays or built-in wardrobes. This should give you the total square metreage you'll need, but you can always use calculators online to work out the dimensions precisely.

Remove the old carpet and underlay. Clear the space of all furniture and lift everything off the floor. Wear protective gear from this point on – gloves, knee pads, a dust mask and protective goggles are advisable. The carpet is held in place by carpet grippers along the edge of the room, so pick a corner, grab the carpet with a pair of pliers, and pull. If it doesn't come up easily, cut a small section with a utility knife, and then pull it up by hand. Repeat the same process for the underlay. Waste carpet is accepted at most recycling waste depots so you should be able to take your old carpet and underlay to your local tip.

Toni's Top Tip

It's always worth adding a bit extra on to your measurements in case of any problems. It's also really handy to keep some offcuts to use at a later point if you need to spot-test the carpet for cleaning stains (see page 31).

Getting rid of carpet gripper

If you aren't replacing the carpet, you'll need to remove the carpet gripper that runs around the edge of the room. You can prise it loose using a claw hammer, chisel or other sharp-edged tool, but take care as it's very spiky. If you're laying vinyl or sanding existing floorboards, you might need to go round the room and fill in nail holes left behind from the gripper with wood filler, then sand down once dry until smooth.

Clean and prep the floor. Sweep and vacuum thoroughly, then smooth out any areas that might be covered with residue or damage from the previous carpet using a sander appropriate for your floor surface. If the floor is uneven concrete, you might want to look at using self-levelling floor screed, or call in a professional if you feel intimidated by this. Once your floor is fully cleaned, prepped and dry, you're ready to fit the carpet gripper strips around the edge of the room. These come in long wooden strips that can be cut to size then nailed, stapled or stuck down using an adhesive suitable for your floor.

Fit the underlay. Roll out the underlay and cut to size. Start from the furthest corner away from the door, stretch and either nail or staple the underlay to wooden floors using a nail or staple gun, or use flooring adhesive suitable for concrete floors. Staple together any seams of the underlay as well, or use gaffer tape to join them. Repeat this process until the entire surface is covered and use offcuts to fill any small gaps.

Lay the carpet. Before cutting the carpet to size, make sure you double check your measurements and calculations, leaving a few centimetres of excess at the edges. Make sure that the pile of any carpet pieces you may need to cut for awkward spaces can be laid in the same direction as the main section of carpet.

Once you're happy with the alignment, cut to size and lay out over the underlay. Then, go over the carpet with both feet in a shuffling motion to flatten any bunching. Follow the instructions from your stretcher and tucker to attach the carpet to the gripper. Trim the carpet with your knife, ensuring you've left enough to tuck it into the edges of the room, but not so much that it bunches. Place the stretcher against the carpet and push it with your knee to stretch the carpet into the gripper strips, working your way around the room to ensure the carpet is fitted snugly.

Clean up. Vacuum the whole of the carpet to remove stray bits of fluff, then sit back and enjoy the results of your hard work.

> Laying Laminate Flooring

We've ticked off carpet, now let's look at wooden flooring, with laminate in particular being a great way to get the wood-floor look with added durability. Best of all, it's quite straightforward to lay yourself. That being said, nothing is ever that easy, and there are a few key things to bear in mind before you get started.

Different types of laminate have different locking mechanisms, so do your research before you buy. As a general rule, rapid-fit is quicker and easier to lay, particularly if you're working alone. Your flooring must always be fitted in accordance with the manufacturer's guidelines, but there are a few basic tips that will help you regardless of the type.

ALLOW TIME FOR . . .

- **The laminate flooring strips to acclimatize to the room – at least 48 hours**
- **The floor to cure for after installation – at least 24 hours**

WHAT YOU NEED

- Tape measure
- Pencil
- Underlay suitable for your floor
- Knee pads
- Large strong scissors
- Laminate flooring boards
- Trim (optional)
- Spirit level
- Spacers
- Jigsaw
- Mop, bucket and floor-cleaning fluid
- Planer (optional)

HOW TO

1   Calculate the overall area of your room to determine how many packs of flooring and underlay you'll need. Measure the length and width of the space at the widest point, using your tape measure. Work in mm ((length x width) ÷ 1000) = number of metres squared) and remember to include any alcoves. When buying laminate, always get packs from the same batch for consistency. It's a good idea to buy an extra pack or two of flooring to allow for errors during laying, and in case any strips need replacing in the future.

2   The total thickness of the underlay and flooring also needs to be calculated as this will affect whether your doors will still be able to open smoothly. If the new flooring is higher than the original floor the doors and architrave may need to be planed.

3 As with carpet, it's recommended that you fit underlay beneath your laminate flooring to provide stability and support to the boards as well as sound insulation. The type of underlay will be determined by your subfloor, but it will likely be foam or fibreboard. Foam is ideal for making floors seem even more cushioned, fibreboard is ideal for cold floors such as ground floors or cellars as it is thermally insulating. If you are laying on concrete, you will need to use underlay with a damp-proof membrane as concrete releases moisture, which can damage laminate.

4 You need to store laminate flooring in the room it will be fitted in up to 48 hours before laying it, to allow it to acclimatize to the room's temperature and humidity, so put the unopened packs in the room a few days before you start work. Proper prep helps to guarantee a longer lifespan for your new flooring, so don't skip this step.

5 Prep your space by removing any existing flooring and underlay (see page 58), and ensure all existing floorboards are firmly secured with no nails or screws sticking out. Then vacuum, mop clean and allow the floor to dry thoroughly.

6 Rows of underlay should be laid perpendicular to the laminate, so decide which way you'd like your laminate to run before you lay your underlay (see page 59). If you're laying laminate over concrete, you'll need to lay polyethylene or polypropylene underlay to ensure no moisture will leak from the concrete into the laminate. Always check the underlay is suitable for your floor before buying it.

7 Your laminate boards can be laid either lengthways or widthways, but it's best to set out some boards before making a commitment to see which arrangement best suits your room. That being said, if you're laying the laminate on top of existing floorboards, you'll need to lay the new flooring perpendicular to the boards to ensure it's stable.

8 Laminate also needs to be laid with an expansion gap of 10–12mm around the edges of the room as the boards swell and contract over time. Be sure to check the manufacturer's guidelines for your product. If your existing skirting boards are at least that thick, carefully remove them prior to fitting the laminate and reinstall the skirting boards once the flooring is in place. An easier approach is to fit flooring trim to conceal the gap between the laminate and the existing skirting.

9 Measure, mark and cut the boards as necessary to fit the space using a jigsaw.

10 Start at a straight wall and lay your first row, joining all the edge boards. If you like, you can use spacers to help ensure you maintain a 10mm gap from the wall.

11 Continue this process until you reach the other side of the room, making sure you have an expansion gap around the edges.

12 Once you've finished laying the laminate floor, you need to let it cure, meaning you mustn't walk on it for 24 hours after installation as doing so could damage the installation, leaving you with an uneven floor – the last thing you want after all your hard work!

Furniture

Furniture is a great way to express your unique personal taste through different styles, colours and finishes. It can be a significant investment, so you don't necessarily want to replace key items more often than you have to. Luckily, there are so many ways you can extend the life of a beloved piece of furniture with your imagination and a bit of DIY elbow grease. If you're ever stumped for an idea, visit the DIY OAB group for some inspiration.

> Upcycling Furniture

You might be looking at the same old bits of furniture and thinking you can't wait to see the back of them but you really can't afford to replace them right now. Sometimes we can all be too quick to think that the answer to our sad and battered furniture is to chuck it all out and buy shiny new replacements, but an alternative solution might be right under your nose . . .

Upcycling is a fantastic option for many reasons. It's fun, you can learn some new skills, it's usually cheaper than buying new, you can let your creativity flow and it's kinder to the environment because fewer items of unwanted furniture end up in landfill. Best of all, what have you got to lose? If it goes wrong, change it. Start again.

There's so much you can do to give furniture another lease on life – the only limit is your imagination. In this section are a few ideas and techniques that you can try, which require no previous skills or expertise.

Upcycling dos and don'ts

Whether it's painting something afresh or changing the fixtures and fittings, there are a few things to bear in mind before you let your inner DIY queen loose . . .

Do . . .

- Prep your area. If you're going to be upcycling a wooden item, or doing any sort of painting, make sure you put down some dust sheets or newspaper to protect the surfaces where you're working. If you are upcycling a fireplace, for example, tape off any areas you don't want to damage, such as walls.

- Make sure you have everything you need before you start. If you're painting, check you have enough paint, as well as enough paint brushes, rollers and sandpaper. If you're planning on trying a technique such as decoupage, or you're going to stick new materials onto your furniture, make sure you have the right adhesive (see Toni's Top Tip on page 70) and enough of whatever it is you're adding. It's always better to have too much than too little.

- Go bold. If you're upcycling a cabinet, for example, try out a vibrant colour or some new handles and knobs. This is your chance to develop your own style, so be brave.

Don't . . .

- Start without a plan. Upcycling can be a lot of fun, but even if you aren't entirely sure how you want the end product to look, make sure you have at least an idea of what you want to do. Do some research online, watch some tutorials, and don't go in totally unprepared.

- Be lazy when it comes to wood. The more you prep the surface, the better your project will turn out. So make sure to sand it well, then vacuum and wipe it down with a damp cloth before using a primer, which will help the new coat of paint to stick.

- Use the wrong tools. As with the prep, make sure you have the right tools for the job before you get started.

Toni's Top Tip

Coffee granules mixed to a concentrated paste or a dark-brown shoe polish are both great options for covering scratches on furniture and wooden floors – simply apply liberally with a cloth and wipe away any excess.

Upcycling Top Tips

1   Be imaginative when looking for ways to upcycle: use a ladder to display plants and photos, and wooden crates as shelves or storage boxes that are functional and attractive.

2   Always make sure the item of furniture is structurally sound – there's no point in spending time and materials on a woodworm-riddled sofa that will fall apart when you sit on it. Be realistic about how much repair work you are willing and able to do.

3   As always, preparation is all-important, so try to plan ahead. This could include making rough sketches, double checking what tools you need, or just giving your second-hand/vintage find a good clean.

4   If you're applying wax to wooden furniture, old socks make a great (and cheap) applicator. As long as they aren't too fluffy, they'll work wonders.

5   If you're not sure where to start, check out the DIY OAB group for ideas, or platforms such as Pinterest to get your creative juices flowing.

6   Our community knows that sometimes DIY and upcycling can be intimidating, but just go for it – you'll be chuffed once you're done, and you'll be proud that you have something utterly unique and personal! Mistakes are inevitable but they aren't something to be sad or mad about – each one is a lesson learned. You'll get better and braver the more projects you take on!

> Personalizing Your Item with Stencils

One way to ensure a makeover is really personal is through the use of stencils. They're a simple and cheap way to restyle an item of furniture, storage boxes or even wooden frames. You can find all kinds of stencils online, especially ones of animals or flowers for children's bedrooms, or you can make your own by printing off a template from the internet. Whatever design you choose, they're all so easy to apply.

Here we'll take you through how to add a wonderful stencil design to a chest of drawers, but the principle is pretty much the same whichever item of furniture you decide to work with.

ALLOW TIME FOR . . .

- Paint to dry

WHAT YOU NEED

- Dust sheets
- Clean damp cloth
- Non-stripping cleaning product (optional)
- Paint (we recommend chalk paint)
- Paint brush
- Stencil
- Masking tape
- Sealer of your choice (we recommend soft wax, but check it's compatible with the paint you've chosen)

HOW TO

1 First, lay down the dust sheets in the area where you're working – an even better option is to do projects like this outside so you don't risk any damage to the rest of your home.

2 You'll need to prepare the chest of drawers before you get started with the stencils. Rub down the surfaces with a clean damp cloth and, if it's particularly dirty, use a non-stripping cleaning product to remove any grease or residue.

3 Test your paint on an inconspicuous area and leave it to dry.

4 Carefully consider where you'll be placing the stencil – will the pattern be on the drawers only or across the entire item? Once you've decided on the position, use masking tape to secure the stencil to the surface.

5 Start with your first coat of paint. Remember, you don't need to achieve full coverage first time around, and it's better to do two coats of paint for a really strong look (but always check the instructions on the tin). Leave the stencil taped in place between coats and allow the paint to dry fully before moving on to the next step.

6 Now you can seal the paint using wax, according to the instructions on the tin. Let the entire piece dry and you're all done.

> Dip into Decoupage

If you want to bring your furniture to life with a bit of an out-there idea and you're feeling brave, decoupage could be the project for you.

So, what is it? Decoupage involves decorating an object by gluing coloured-paper cut-outs onto it in combination with special paint effects, gold leaf and other decorative elements. It's a really versatile technique that can be used widely around the home – on anything from kitchen cabinets to table tops, furniture, lampshades and vases. It's a brilliant way to show off your creative side and bring your personality into your home.

You can use pretty much any kind of paper – tear out images from magazines or newspapers, or use wrapping paper, wallpaper, paper napkins, doilies, playing cards, crafting paper or even fabric.

Toni's Top Tip

You can buy brand-name all-in-one sealer, glue and finish that will dry clear and hold your chosen paper pieces tight for a textured finish, but this can be expensive. A cheaper alternative is slightly watered-down PVA glue.

ALLOW TIME FOR . . .

- The adhesive to dry completely – at least 48 hours

WHAT YOU NEED

- Dust sheets
- Fine-grit (120) sandpaper
- Clean damp cloth
- Primer (optional)
- Paint brushes
- Scissors
- PVA glue
- Craft paint brushes
- Paper or fabric of your choice
- Lacquer or varnish

HOW TO

1   Prepare your workspace – this can get messy, so make sure you put down some dust sheets to protect the area you're working on, or carry out the project outside.

2   Prepare the item of furniture – if it's made of wood, give it a sand, clean it, then prime it if you want to apply your decoupage to a coloured surface. Allow it to dry thoroughly before you start getting crafty!

3   Choose the material you want to use – we've made some suggestions on the previous page but you can use a wide range of materials. Be daring!

4 Tear or cut up the material – you might want to be very precise if you're going for a uniform style, but for a more rustic look, you could just rip it up so the pieces overlap.

5 Pour some glue into a pot, dip in your brush, then coat the back of your first piece of material and press it onto your item of furniture. (If you're decoupaging a large object, use the brush to spread the glue directly onto the item rather than the material to save time.)

6 Continue to decoupage until you've used up all of your material; you don't have to wait for the individual pieces to dry before you apply more. Once you've completed your design, leave it to dry for up to 48 hours.

7 The final stage is to seal your item. Spread a thin layer of lacquer or varnish over the entire piece of furniture. This will protect it and ensure everything stays in place.

Toni's Top Tips

Always, always seal. This is a step that cannot be missed out, otherwise your design will eventually peel off or get damaged.

Ripped-up old sheets and bedding can work just as well as paper and will add some texture to your design.

Watch Out!

There are three things in the whole house that DIYers should only ever attempt with extreme caution – plumbing, electrics and structural work. (Anything involving gas is strictly off limits as you must be registered to work on gas fittings.) If in doubt, always consult a professional. In the UK, even if you feel confident enough to carry out these tasks yourself, they will need to be signed off by a professional in the event that, for example, you want to sell your house. More importantly, they're dangerous, so always proceed with caution.

Halls, Stairs and Landings

There isn't a day goes by when you don't pass through these areas of your home. Given the heavy foot traffic as well as kids dragging their bikes and bags, and pets charging around these central thoroughfares, marks, scuffs, knocks, scratches and dents are inevitable. When you're thinking about redecorating, your halls, stairs and landing might be at the bottom of the list, not least because it feels like such a big job to navigate, with high ceilings, bannisters and stair treads to consider, and multiple doorways leading to rooms with different flooring or different wall colours. It all seems too complicated!

We want to show you that it's not as daunting as it might appear at first, and that you can transform the whole vibe of your home by spending a bit of time on these areas. The hallway is often the first thing you, or anyone else, sees when entering your home, so you can make a real statement here. A boldly coloured staircase, some practical yet chic panelling on the walls, some patterned flooring or a statement light – whatever you choose to do can have a big impact in creating that fabulous first impression when you open the front door, and might really change the way you think about your home.

Best of all, because most of us don't have large hallways and landings, it's unlikely that you'll need to spend much money on furniture (not many of us have room for a three-seater sofa on the landing!), so a makeover here should cost a lot less than other rooms in the house.

This section contains everything you could want to know about how to get more for less. From mixing colours or shapes on your bannister and how best to fill the staircase space, to doors and that all-important hardwearing skirting, whatever you're planning, we've got it covered.

> Bannisters

Those of you with staircases and bannisters in your home will know that, over time, they can really start to show the wear and tear of daily life. Mucky hands on the walls, moving furniture while negotiating the stairs . . . whatever the culprit, a few knocks can mean chipped and scuffed paintwork, loose handrails and even missing spindles. Here's a mix of ideas to revitalize your bannisters and make your hallway look top notch.

New paint job

A fresh lick of paint will help bring a bannister back to life, particularly if yours is white, as lighter colours can fade or yellow over time. Make sure to use a suitable wood paint for the job (see page 81).

Add a splash of colour

What about a dramatic change? You could go for a bold contrast to the woodwork or walls, or paint the spindles and handrail a different colour, or even pick a different colour for each spindle. There have been some really striking rainbow bannisters shared to the DIY OAB group.

Go black and white

A two-tone bannister can introduce a luxury hotel vibe to your space.

Change your spindles

Bored with your plain wooden spindles? Mix it up with some new ones that are turned or shaped, or consider using a different material – wrought iron, or even Perspex or glass, for a solid but transparent modern alternative.

Replace your handrail

Just as with spindles, there's a wide variety of handrails out there, many of which can be really affordable. Go for slimline and discreet, or make a statement with a flat and chunky rail. Perhaps your style is traditional or more modern?

Think horizontal

The majority of staircase bannisters have vertical spindles, but going horizontal with them can produce a really modern look. Be warned that if you have children, this style is very tempting for them to use as a climbing frame, so it might be a look that's safer with older, less adventurous individuals.

Go glass

Understandably, this route can be more expensive, but fitting glass panels in the gaps between your newel posts at either end of your staircase can look really special. That being said, glass does mean sticky finger marks and lots of cleaning!

Toni's Top Tip

For a really easy way to paint turned bannister rails and spindles, try the sock method, which went viral on the DIY OAB group! Pop a disposable plastic glove on your hand and then cover it with an old sock. Dip the sock into the paint and then rub it over the part of the staircase you want to paint. It gives a really even coverage in a fraction of the time it takes to use a brush!

> Painting Stairs

A fresh coat of paint is the easiest way to revitalize your staircase. While it's a fairly straightforward job that you can do over the course of a weekend, you must ensure the stairs are in good condition before you start painting, and you must prepare them appropriately.

Let's run through some tips and a few style pointers that you may not have considered.

Style ideas

- **White and bright.** White is the most common colour for bannisters and staircases, and it's easy to see why. It's classic, simple, brightens any space, and doesn't fight against any other colours you might have on the walls or carpet.

- **Bold and vibrant.** If you have a neutral colour on your walls, why not go for something really bright and bold on your bannister? Striking yellow or royal blue, perhaps? Seeing a burst of colour first thing in the morning just might get your day off to an upbeat start, or cheer you up when you step through the front door after a long day at work.

- **Chic two-tone.** Painting the riser of each step a dark grey or deep navy, then leaving the tread as natural wood, or white, will give your stairs a really modern and sharp look.

- **Gradient steps.** Can't settle on a particular shade of blue or green? Why not go for all of them? Paint your first step a darker shade of one colour, then progress to a lighter shade with every step upwards to create a relaxing sense of calm.

- **Stencil it up.** Why stick to block colours? Stencils can be a really cheap and great way to add geometric prints, mock-tile patterns or perhaps a floral design to your stair treads. Shop around online for some inspiration, and see page 68 for top tips for successful stencil applications.

- **Personalize each step.** DIY OAB members have created some really striking staircase designs using inspirational quotes, names of family members or other personalized text. If you don't have a steady hand, you can have letter stencils, or even full phrases, made up by companies online, which will make the process even easier.

- **Painted runner.** A carpeted runner can add a touch of luxury to your staircase, but if your budget doesn't stretch to new carpet, why not create the look by painting a bold contrasting colour in the middle two-thirds of the treads and risers, running up the stairs, leaving a lighter colour for the edges.

Toni's Top Tip

Painting a staircase isn't a quick job, so if you don't have time to do it all in one go, try breaking it down into stages. Maybe do the spindles one day and the handrail another, or half the bannisters, then the other half. It's worth bearing in mind that if you do the spindles first, you won't have to tape off the floor and wall.

> How to Paint a Staircase

Once you've decided on your new look, it's time to get cracking. It can be quite overwhelming to look at all that fiddly woodwork, as well as the walls and ceilings, so here are a few tips to help you manage the project without running out of steam!

Pick the right paint

Regardless of your colour scheme, make sure you have the right type of paint for the job. Most paint companies manufacture their own specialist floor paints, which you can use for the treads. The good news is that you don't need a primer with many of them, thanks to the high binder content in the formulation. Make sure your paint can withstand heavy traffic, and is washable, for easy cleaning of all those mucky hand- and footprints. Water-based paints dry much quicker than oil-based paints, so can be painted again in a shorter amount of time. They also won't yellow with age.

Pick the right time

First up, it's best to choose a day when everyone is out of the house or, at the very least, a time when you can prevent any little footprints or handprints from marking your fresh coat.

Prep your space

Cover any surfaces you don't want painted. Use dust sheets or tape them up using painter's tape.

Prep the stairs

Hammer in or remove any nails, or tighten any screws that are protruding. If there are any dents or areas that you want to level out, fill them in with some wood filler and allow to dry. Next, lightly sand all the woodwork so that it's free from lumps and bumps and the new paint has something to adhere to. Make sure you vacuum all the surfaces thoroughly, then wipe them down with a clean damp cloth. For a thorough clean, use some sugar soap before wiping down the area one final time and allowing it to dry.

Prime the wood

This isn't an essential step on already painted wood, or if you're painting the treads with a specialist floor paint, but it will help you achieve a better finish on the spindles and handrails. It will also help if you're going for a lighter colour. Make sure to buy a wood primer that's suitable for stairs and, once the paint is dry, rub any bumps or drips with sandpaper to smooth the surface, then wipe away any dust with a damp cloth.

Time to paint

Start from the top of the staircase – it'll make your life a lot easier. Paint around the edges of the stairs first with a paint brush, then use a roller for a smooth finish on the treads and risers. Use a smaller roller for precision, or see the sock tip on page 78 for an even easier method to paint the spindles and handrail. If you think it needs it, and given the amount of traffic on most staircases, it probably does, then follow the manufacturer's guidelines for a second coat.

Finishing touches

Remove any tape and coverings, give everything a final clean and enjoy!

Toni's Top Tip

When using painter's tape, run a damp cloth over it before painting to activate the gel in the tape. This will form a strong seal to achieve crisp lines with no bleeding. Always remove the tape while the final coat of paint is still wet and, for a cleaner removal, peel it back on itself rather than at a 90-degree angle.

> Wall Panelling

You've probably noticed how popular wall panelling has become, so you'll be pleased to know it's a look you can easily achieve yourself. There are different approaches to wall panelling, such as the sleek, modern grand design look or more traditional tongue-and-groove pattern. In this section we'll talk through a step-by-step guide to the grand design style, but most of the directions can be applied to other patterns too. You could do one wall of your hallway as a statement, or every wall along your hall, stairs and landing for an overall refresh. It's a particularly useful wall covering for these areas as it protects the plaster from the inevitable knocks and chips.

It's a good idea to get some inspirational images of the panelling pattern you want to achieve, perhaps even making a rough sketch in the space provided at the end of this chapter. This will help with the next steps.

ALLOW TIME FOR . . .

- **The adhesive to dry**

WHAT YOU NEED

- **Decorator's caulk/acrylic filler (optional)**
- **Sandpaper (with or without an electric sander)**
- **Tape measure**
- **Notebook and pencil**
- **Spirit level**
- **MDF wood panelling**
- **Jigsaw**
- **Laser level**
- **Heavy-duty glue**
- **Hammer and nails**
- **Paint**
- **Paint brush and roller**

HOW TO

1 As we've established, planning and preparation are key to any successful DIY project. Make sure to prepare the wall you're going to apply the panelling to by removing any existing fixtures, filling any holes and smoothing with sandpaper once dry.

2 Next, start measuring. Take your time and always double check your figures. Use the tape measure to make note of the full width and height of the entire wall. Decide how many panels you want – are you doing a half wall or the full wall? The number of panels you decide upon should include the base, top, vertical and horizontal panels.

3 Once you've bought the MDF you need for your panel design, measure out the size of your panels on the MDF, mark where to cut them using a pencil, then use your saw to cut the panels to the size you need. Ideally, do this step outside to avoid getting MDF dust in your home.

4 Using a pencil and a spirit level, mark the wall to indicate where the panels will go.

5 First add the frame – these are the panels that sit on the outer edges of the wall, which are the base panels and top panels. You can use a laser level to check your panels are straight.

6 Apply heavy-duty glue to the back of the panels and press them gently but firmly against the wall. You can use both nails and glue, although glue should suffice.

7 Next, move on to your vertical panels and repeat the process. Use your spirit level to check they're straight and aligned at the top. Follow up with the horizontal panels.

8 Once you've applied all your panels to the wall, use the filler to fill any gaps. If the filler leaves any lumps, use the sandpaper to smooth them away.

9 Finally, when your glue and filler have dried completely, it's time to get painting. We love chic inky blues or forest greens, but the choice is yours!

> Doors

Let's face it, there are doors to be found even in the most open-plan homes, and they're a particularly prominent feature of hallways and landings. Internal doors are sometimes forgotten in DIY planning, and the styling possibilities can be overlooked. They're often neglected because they can be notoriously expensive and fiddly to replace, but there are some great DIY projects to transform them without too much expense.

Toni's Top Tip

Some people find it easier to paint a door when it's taken off its hinges. If you have space, take down the door, remove all the hinges and handles, pop it onto a sawhorse or table, and paint one side at a time. Rehang once it's dry.

Paint

If you're looking for a quick and simple refresh to give your home a more contemporary, clean look, a fresh coat of white paint on your doors could be the solution you're looking for. There's an almost infinite number of shades of white, but whichever one you go for will result in an effortless uplift and will increase the feeling of light in any room or doorway.

Switch handles

It could be time for a switch-out, to change those outdated door handles for some on-trend ones. This is the easiest option by far to upgrade your doors, and it can make a real impact. Depending on which handles you go for, it can be the cheapest option too. There are hundreds of styles of handles out there, so it's really about picking the ones that reflect the look you want to achieve. It's worth having matching handles for all your doors, but if it's too expensive to do that straight away, consider doing this in stages, and changing the fittings on a group of doors near to each other each time.

Create panels

Plain doors can feel bland – you might look at them and feel that something is missing. A current trend that helps to solve this problem is adding panels to them using mouldings, which can add detail and a luxury feel (see below).

> Moulding

This DIY idea ticks every box: it's easy, inexpensive and transformative, giving some dimension and interest to an otherwise boring surface. To add mouldings or trimmings to a door, you don't even need to take the door off the hinges, and it'll only take a couple of hours. It's that simple.

ALLOW TIME FOR . . .

- Paint to dry between coats
- Glue for mouldings to dry

WHAT YOU NEED

- Pencil and long ruler
- Wall/cabinet trim moulding strips
- Safety goggles
- Handsaw or jigsaw
- Dust sheet
- Primer
- Paint brush
- Gloss paint (this can match your existing door colour or you can pick a contrasting shade for the moulding strips)
- Heavy-duty wood glue or hot glue with a glue gun

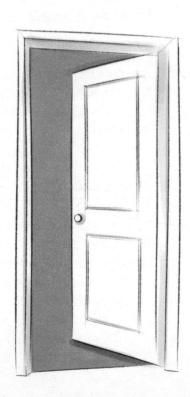

HOW TO

1   Use a long ruler and pencil to measure and mark where you want to position your mouldings on the door. Usually, placing the mouldings around 10–12cm from the edges of the door will work nicely, but make sure the distance is equal on both sides and on the top and bottom too. Measure, measure, measure!

2   Measure the lengths of all the lines you have drawn on the door and add them up so you know the total length of mouldings you need. Make sure to add a little extra to allow for trimming each piece to size.

3   Measure the moulding strips to the length you need, marking the cut points with a pencil.

4   Time to pop on your safety goggles to cut the mouldings with your handsaw or jigsaw. Remember to cut the ends of the mouldings at 45-degree angles so that you can join them at the corners.

5   Lay the moulding strips on a dust sheet and paint their entire surface with primer. Allow to dry, then apply a layer of gloss. Allow to dry once more, then paint a final coat, if needed, leaving that to dry too.

6   Now it's time to add your mouldings to the door. Apply a bead of glue along the length of the markings in preparation for the mouldings. If you're using hot glue, be ready to press the mouldings onto the door straight away, as the glue can dry quickly. Don't apply too much, as it will only ooze out from the sides and create a messy finish.

7 Repeat with all the pieces and leave to dry. Your door is now looking better than ever, for very little money and time!

Toni's Top Tip

Combine a few of the DIY door projects listed above for a whole new style – try painting the door and mouldings a new colour, then swap out the handles too. You'll be amazed at the difference a few changes can make.

> Fitting Skirting Boards

Skirting boards might not be your most urgent DIY project, but they can be a cheap and quick change that can give any room a little boost. They're also a really useful addition to a room to complete the overall look and bear the brunt of any scrapes and knocks to the walls as you push back furniture. Skirting board uplifts can range from a lick of paint to fitting completely new ones, but the clever trick below takes away all the mess and effort of replacing them, by simply covering them with fresh, clean boards.

WHAT YOU NEED

- Clean damp cloth
- Ruler/tape measure

- **Skirting board covers (typically MDF)**
- **Pencil**
- **Safety goggles**
- **Handsaw or jigsaw**
- **Heavy-duty glue**
- **Pin nailer or nail gun**

HOW TO

1   As ever, preparation is very important, so wipe down your existing skirting boards with a clean damp cloth and allow to dry. You want them to be as clean as possible so that the glue creates a firm bond between the two boards.

2   Measure the existing skirting boards with the tape measure so you know the length, height and depth for each section and therefore how much to buy.

3   Once you have the skirting covers, use a pencil and ruler to measure and mark the point for cutting. Pop on your goggles, then cut your new skirting covers to size with your handsaw or jigsaw, so that they are the appropriate length – they should slot perfectly over the existing boards.

4   At this point, you're ready to secure the board. You can use heavy-duty glue, but the ideal way is to use both glue and a pin nailer or nail gun.

5   That's it! You now have new skirting boards – all without hours of ripping and prying the old ones off the wall.

Toni's Top Tip

Adding skirting board covers provides a great opportunity to do some sneaky organization and decluttering – hide wires and telephone or television cables in the gap between the existing boards and the new covers!

> Filling the Space

The hallway can be a busy space, but it's also a pretty important one that deserves your attention. Just because it needs to be functional doesn't mean it has to be bland, messy or boring. You can still add life, character and style with your design choices. Here are some ideas for making the most of this space.

Walls (wallpaper/paint)

It can be said for every room, but it's also true for your hallway – your walls don't have to be plain and you don't have to play it safe. The addition of colour can take your hallway from blah to beautiful – see the painting section on page 18 for more tips and inspiration.

A popular choice for hallway makeovers is wallpaper, but my advice is not to wallpaper your entire hallway. Try doing just one wall alongside a complementary paint colour and you'll create an inviting space with a focal point that's magazine-worthy.

Storage

Coats. Shoes. Hats. Gloves. Bags. Scarves. Wallets. Leashes. The list goes on and on. Maximize your hallway storage by utilizing any space you have, especially if you have kids or pets. Smart storage solutions can sometimes look utilitarian or cold, but you can find plenty of inspiration online and within the DIY OAB community that is both useful and attractive.

If you're really short on space, try a vertical solution, such as a shelving unit that attaches to the wall and doesn't take up valuable floor space. Adding more items might feel counterintuitive but you can avoid that cluttered look by using baskets and boxes that slot neatly into spaces and are filled up with all your bits and pieces – hampers and woven baskets are particularly on trend. Finally, remember to use the space under your stairs, whether that's building a miniature coat cupboard or fitting a bench where you can sit and put on your shoes (or wait for your teenagers). This space is very versatile (see page 266)!

Lighting

Light helps to create an atmosphere, and makes your hallway feel warm, welcoming and cosy. Depending on the size and shape of your entrance hall, you can try a ceiling light fitting that looks like a piece of art itself and bounces the light around what might otherwise be a dark and small space – think pendant lamps, bright colours, patterned glassware or modern chandeliers. If you have the sockets and enough space, a lamp on a side table will give off a soft, inviting glow in the evenings, especially if you pick a lightbulb with a warm tone rather than bright white. Some people even opt to run small spotlights along the edge of their hallway skirting boards, a style better suited to particularly long and dark hallways, or up the edge of stair treads and risers. All you'll need is some stick-on LED sensor lights, a plug socket near by and less than an hour of your afternoon.

Art

To bring some personality to your hallway, try creating your own gallery wall. Art prints in chic frames can provide colour, pattern or intrigue and look great going up the wall next to your stairs. The choice of pieces can be tailored to your taste by picking prints that you love – go for colourful quotes, abstract designs or a full monochrome look, using black-and-white family photos. A gallery wall should look cohesive but not overly uniform, so experiment with displaying them at different heights and use a variety of frames that fit within your chosen theme (see page 160 for tips on hanging pictures).

Mirrors

Beyond the obvious practical benefits, such as reflecting light and adding depth to a small space, a mirror can also be a handy hallway addition for a last-minute make-up or outfit check as you head out the door or before you welcome someone into your home. Something stuck in your teeth? Ladder in your tights? We've all been there. A large mirror will give a full-length view and can sit on the floor and run to the ceiling, or a smaller mirror – perhaps a vintage find with ornate detailing – can sit above a hall table or a radiator. For a DIY project, buy a number of hexagonal mirror pieces and arrange them in a pattern to create a larger mirror, or get a few small square mirrors and place them together using painted wood to build a frame to create a glazed window frame effect.

> <u>Living Features</u>

It's all about bringing the outdoors in right now – indoor plants are definitely having a moment, with vertical and hanging displays trending. Did you know houseplants not only look good but are also proven to boost your mood? There are plants and pots to complement every home's aesthetic, with options for those who are green-fingered goddesses to those who are professional plant-killers. In this section, we'll discuss whether you should opt for artificial or real, and how to create your own DIY living wall.

Real vs artificial

It's an ongoing debate – some of us love the look and feel of a real plant and some of us can't stand the amount of maintenance they require. So here's a breakdown of the pros and cons of real plants and artificial ones.

Real Plants

Pros

Science shows that real plants in a home have a therapeutic effect and can reduce stress levels.

Living plants can help to improve indoor air quality, and flowering ones can make your home look and smell great.

Cons

Real plants can attract pests if they're not cared for properly, the most common being fungus gnats, which are tiny black flies.

If you're an excellent plant parent, keep in mind that your plant may grow, and grow and grow. You may end up having to find a new pot *and* a new spot for it.

Artificial Plants

Pros

Artificial plants are as low maintenance as it gets.

Pets tend to be curious and can be allergic to some plants, but artificial ones don't pose any danger to your furry friends.

Cons

Artificial plants are known for collecting dust in between leaves or petals, so you'll need to dust them regularly.

You get what you pay for – some faux plants are flimsy and will fall apart or degrade in colour and shape over time.

> Fitting an Indoor Hanging Basket

These can look great in any room, and by hanging them from the ceiling, a shelf, or the wall you reap all the benefits of interior greenery without sacrificing valuable floor space.

If you're not green-fingered, make things really easy for yourself by purchasing a ready-potted hanging basket from a store – you'll be surprised by the number of budget-friendly options available. Shop around and you'll be sure to find one you love. Then, all you need to do is suspend it from a bracket fixed to the wall or ceiling.

WHAT YOU NEED

- Ceiling hook (curved swag hooks are ideal)
- Pencil
- Tape measure
- Hinged clip (if wall is plasterboard)
- Drill with drill bits
- Rawl plugs
- (Pre-potted) hanging basket

HOW TO

1 Before you go any further, check if your choice of hook has a maximum weight. If it does, compare this weight with that of the hanging basket and plant you selected – real plants weigh more than artificial ones as they also need soil and water, making them much heavier.

2 Start by marking the ceiling, shelf or surface with a pencil so you know exactly where you want to attach your hook and where you want the plant to hang from. To make sure your hook placement is perfect, it might help to use your tape measure to see how low your basket will hang. You don't want to be hitting your head on it every time you walk past.

3 If you're attaching your hook to a wall made of plasterboard, you'll also need to add a hinged clip, which will anchor the hook on the opposite side of the plasterboard. Once the clip is pushed through the hole you drill, it will open flat against the surface and stop the hook from falling out.

4 Drill the hole, add a rawl plug and screw in your hook, then double and triple check your hook is secure – we don't want hanging baskets falling from above!

5 That's it – suspend your plant from the hook and you have a stylish green addition to your room.

Toni's Top Tips

To save on cleaning up, hold an envelope under the area where you're drilling to catch the dust.

If you want to be really creative, for a more natural look you can use rope to hang your basket. Search online for tips on rope- and knot-tying to add an extra-special DIY touch.

Toni's Top Tip

If you're using real plants, hang them somewhere they can receive plenty of natural light, near a window, but out of draughts. Also, don't hang a basket over a carpeted hallway or landing as watering will create a mess!

Members' Top Tips

- Hanging plants work really well outside, too, attached to fences or walls around dining tables or hot tubs.
- They also work well in a child's bedroom as part of a jungle theme.
- Attach fairy lights to your basket for a pretty night-time effect.

Stair Runners

Toni's Choice

I realize not everyone has a staircase at home, but if you do, a stair runner is a great way to make it really pop, as well as making the treads quieter and less slippery – functionality and style combined. I've chosen group member Ceri Griffiths' project for her honest approach to the task at hand and the incredible result she achieved – this gets a big thumbs-up from me!

ALLOW TIME FOR . . .

- Prepping the stairs by cleaning and sanding
- Allowing time for paint, stain or varnish to dry

WHAT YOU NEED

- Tape measure
- Pencil
- Sandpaper
- Orbital sander (optional)
- Tack cloth and sugar soap
- Wood filler

- Wood stain, varnish or paint (depending on your chosen finish)
- Gripper rods or double-sided carpet tape
- Nails and screws
- Hammer or staple gun
- Cordless drill with drill bits
- Stair rods and brackets
- Tubing cutter
- Stair runner

HOW TO

1 Follow the instructions on page 78 for prepping and painting your stairs before adding the stair runner.

2 Measure the tread – the flat bit you step on – and the riser – the vertical bit that goes up to the next step. If your stairs are straight and evenly sized, you can measure one tread and riser, then multiply that measurement by the total number of steps to work out the overall length of stair runner you'll need. To be on the safe side, you can always measure every step. Allow a bit extra, just in case – you'll always be able to use it in a nook and cranny later.

3 You'll want your stair runner to be centred, so measure the width of the staircase from left to right and divide that number by two to get your centre point. Make a little mark at this centre point on the step.

4 Stair runners are functional as well as decorative and it's essential to fit yours using gripper rods or double-sided carpet tape. Gripper rods come in both medium- and short-pin, depending on the thickness of the carpet being fitted, and you'll need one length of gripper for each riser and one for each tread. Measure and cut the gripper rods or carpet tape to be slightly narrower than the width of your stair runner to make sure they aren't showing after the carpet has been laid. Fix the grippers to the treads and risers with a hammer and nails or double-sided carpet tape – the riser gripper should be about 1cm above the tread and the tread gripper should be about 1cm away from the edge of the riser – then fix the carpet to the stairs by laying it in place and pushing firmly onto the gripper on each step.

5   Measure the stair rod so that it covers the runner fully at the back of the tread, plus 1-2cm more on each side, depending on the width of your stairs and your personal preference. The stair rods should extend beyond the edge of the carpet runner. If the rods need to be cut down in size, make a mark where you need to cut. Then, using your tubing cutter, slice off the end at this mark. It's more time-efficient if you cut all your rods to size before installing them.

6   Now it's time to start installing the stair rods. Starting at the bottom of the stairs, place the base of your first pair of brackets either side of the runner, where the tread joins the riser.

7   Drill one bracket into your step and insert your rod into it. Then, insert the other end of the rod into the other bracket and drill it in place on the other side of the runner. Continue all the way up the stairs until each tread has a stair rod and brackets in place. Then step back and admire your handiwork!

Member's Method

Finally, I finished my hallway. 🙌 I went for the boho vibe, like me and the rest of my house. ⭐ I did the work myself, as a single mum with no husband to help. Sanding and painting the stairs was the worst!! I had blisters for weeks, then a bad flare-up with my back and joints, so I put everything on hold. All worth the tears and tantrums. 😍 Kept this project on a budget, despite splashing out on the stair runner and rods.

Watch Out!

Stair rods are purely decorative – don't be tempted to think you can use them alone to secure your runner. Make sure to use carpet grippers or double-sided tape to attach the runner to the staircase.

Members' Top Tips

- If your stair rods are too long and need trimming to size, a tubing cutter is an inexpensive tool that slices a tube or rod in a circular motion.

- If you've found antique stair rods, they may be missing their brackets. Don't worry as you can buy pairs of brackets separately. Simply match the finish as best you can and choose the closest diameter possible to accommodate your rods. If in doubt, choose the next size up and add foam inserts to prevent the bar from rattling or moving about.

Members' Comments

Beautiful – you should feel very proud x *Annette Collumbell*

I love it. So different x *Lorraine Ddw*

What an amazing job!! Looks amazing!! 😍 Absolutely love this 🖤 *Alana Henry*

Budget and Schedule Planner

Vision: What do you want to achieve?

Start with the end product so you have a clear idea of where you are going. Pictures, sketches and mood boards can help here, and you can refer back to them as you progress and/or use them for motivation.

My Vision

....

....

....

....

....

....

....

....

....

....

Budget

Once you've costed everything you need, start looking for savings wherever possible using the 7 Golden Rules on page 8, including borrowing, reusing, deal-hunting and hiring equipment.

Use the table below to work out your budget.

WHAT YOU NEED	Cost	GOLDEN RULE SAVING OPTION	Savings
	£		£
	£		£
	£		£
	£		£
	£		£
	£		£
	£		£
	£		£
	£		£
TOTAL COST £		TOTAL SAVINGS £	

Total cost – total savings = budget £

Overspend contingency of 10% £

Total £

Schedule

Breaking down your project into tasks and steps can help make larger projects more manageable and less daunting, and can give you a clear path to achieving your goal. If you're short on funds, you can also plan to get to a point where you can enjoy your progress to date while you save towards doing more.

TASKS/STEPS	TARGET COMPLETION DATE
1	
2	
3	
4	
5	
6	
7	
8	
9	
10	

The Kitchen

The heart of any home, if only for one reason – it's where the kettle is (and the wine). Kitchens come in all shapes and sizes, but no matter how big or small the space, it's always one of the most expensive rooms in the house to do any work to. That being said, we've got some great ideas for how you can give the hub of the home a lift without having to rip everything out and start again.

Think your kitchen cupboards have to stay their original colour? Wrong. Think those broken handles are here to stay? Wrong again. Whether it's a bright new colour or some stylish matt-black handles and knobs, your kitchen can be given more of a facelift than you might think.

So before you set about getting quotes for fitting a whole new kitchen, check out our guide to all of the wonderful things you can do to give yours a new look without blowing your budget. We've included some of the really inventive ideas from our group to give you the inspiration you've been looking for, and to set you on your DIY way. Best of all, we've got some expert tips on how to achieve a professional finish and use the space to its best advantage – we'll even share some clever hidden storage ideas.

> Giving Your Cabinets a New Look

A cheap and cheerful way to update your kitchen cabinets is to paint them – it's even a possibility with laminate cupboards if you use the right type of paint. You can do the job yourself, and a tin of cabinet paint isn't very expensive.

Be warned, it isn't a job for a rainy Sunday afternoon. There's a bit of prep required and you might need a few coats of paint, too. So, be patient and allow yourself at least four days for the job, depending on the size of your kitchen.

WHAT YOU NEED

- **Screwdriver – for removing cupboard doors and handles**
- **Painter's tape**
- **Dust sheets**
- **Degreasing cleaning fluid**
- **Clean cloth, ideally microfibre**
- **Fine-grit (120) sandpaper**
- **Paint brush or roller and tray**
- **Primer (if needed)**
- **Suitable paint – furniture or cupboard paint in your preferred colour**

HOW TO

1 First, remove all the cupboard doors by unscrewing their hinges, then remove the handles. It's much easier

to paint on a flat surface – it will reduce the number of runs and drips from the paint, and it will save your arms and shoulders the pain of having to twist around the cupboards. If you're not able to remove the doors, use painter's tape to cover the hinges and any other parts you don't want to paint, because if these get painted, they'll be the first thing to chip. Also see Toni's Top Tip below about holding the door open!

2   Lay the doors on top of dust sheets to protect your work surfaces and/or floors. Give the area that is to be painted a good clean, using a grease-removing cleaner to ensure the surfaces are free of dirt and dust. Leave all the cabinet doors to dry fully.

Toni's Top Tip

If you're painting cupboard doors while they're still in place, try removing the handles before you start, then stick a screwdriver in the hole. This way, it'll be much easier to hold the door in place while painting the edges.

3   Next, sand the doors very lightly with fine-grit (120) sandpaper to make sure the paint can bond to the surface. Run the brush attachment on the vacuum across the doors, if you like, to remove any residual dust, then wipe them down with a damp clean cloth to ensure the area is dust free. Leave again to dry thoroughly.

4 Finally, it's time to start painting. If you want to, start with a coat of primer (see Toni's Top Tip below). Use a paint brush to begin with, to work the paint into any grooves. It's a good idea to do the first two coats this way, and to allow adequate drying time between each one. Use a roller for your final coat for a smoother finish and to reduce the number of visible brush marks. Leave the doors to dry completely before rehanging them (if you removed them) or using them (if you didn't), then step back to enjoy the transformation!

Toni's Top Tip

To prime or not to prime? Not all paint or surfaces need a primer. Some ranges of furniture and cabinet paints are fine without, so always check the manufacturer's guidelines on the tin beforehand.

> What's the Best Paint to Use?

If you're painting laminate doors, choose a specialist multi-purpose paint for wood, melamine and MDF. If the doors you're painting are wooden, you can use any eggshell or interior wood paint. It's well worth thinking carefully about what you want the finished look to be, too. Paint comes in a varierty of finishes, so decide which one you'd like – from a practical point of view, a satin finish is easier to clean when it gets dirty. Chalk paint is a chic-looking alternative, but if you want your cupboard surfaces to be wipeable, you'll need to seal the top coat with a wax or varnish.

Tips for choosing paint

- If you're unsure about anything, always read the label on the tin of paint – all your questions should be answered there. If not, ask a member of staff at the store where you're purchasing it.

- Some brands of cupboard paint offer small free or inexpensive tester pots, so try before you buy a large tin, to ensure you're happy with the colour on your units.

- All paint takes time to cure – just how long that is varies between types of paints and from brand to brand. Depending on the brand or finish, you might also need to apply several coats to build up the layers of colour.

- Drying times should also be stated on the tin, so ensure you leave enough time for the doors to dry before you reattach them to your units (if you removed them) or use them (if you didn't) to avoid stains and chips.

Toni's Top Tip

An easy way to change the style of your kitchen is to replace the handles and drawer pulls. You can go from modern to traditional or vice versa, choose colours that contrast with the units, or even make them all different for a truly original look.

> **Wrapping Units**

If you don't fancy painting your units, another really effective way to give them a refresh is to wrap them. This trend boomed in the DIY OAB group as it's a brilliant option for anyone on a shoestring budget.

Quite simply, wrapping involves covering surfaces with an adhesive sheet of vinyl. That's it! Vinyl coverings have come a long way since we used to use them to cover our school books, and you can now choose from a huge range of colours, designs and finishes (matt, satin or gloss). With so many designs available, it's a chance to show off your creativity and personality.

Vinyl's toughness and durability make it a perfect material to use in the kitchen. It can also be removed easily, so is a clever option if you're renting somewhere, or if you decide to change the colour.

The numerous features and surfaces it can be used on include:

- Walls and wall panels
- Tiles
- Glass
- Kitchen cabinets and drawer fronts
- Doors
- Work surfaces

ALLOW TIME FOR . . .

- **The adhesive to bond – 48 hours**

YOU WILL NEED

- Tape measure
- Screwdriver – for removing cupboard doors and handles
- Degreasing cleaning fluid
- Clean damp cloth
- Vinyl sheets in the design of your choice
- Scissors
- Clean dry cloth, old loyalty card or vinyl application kit

HOW TO

1   First, measure up all the surfaces in your kitchen that you want to cover to make sure you buy enough vinyl. Allow a centimetre or so extra for it to wrap around the edges of all those surfaces. It's always a good idea to buy a bit extra anyway, in case of errors in the measurements or during the application process! Some vinyl brands include a handy guide on their packaging to assist with this step, or you can find an online guide.

2   Remove any cupboard door handles and remove the doors themselves if you prefer.

3   Use a clean damp cloth to clean all the surfaces you're going to be covering, to ensure they're grease and dust free. Leave them to dry.

4   Cut the approximate size of vinyl you need, then pull back 10cm of the backing paper and apply the vinyl to the surface of your first cupboard door.

5   Using your applicator, an old loyalty card or a clean dry cloth, gently rub over the surface in one direction and keep pulling off the backing paper until the vinyl is fully applied and there are no air bubbles beneath the surface. If you make a mistake, simply pull the vinyl off and start again – it takes 48 hours for the adhesive to bond fully, so you have plenty of time to get it right.

6   As you wrap around any corners, cut a diagonal line into the vinyl to make this process simple and to minimize any puckering.

7   Once the area has been wrapped and sealed, cut away any excess vinyl with a pair of scissors.

Toni's Top Tip

For the best results, invest in an application kit and make full use of the measuring grid on the backing paper. Heating the vinyl with a hair dryer will make it more flexible and easier to work with, which is particularly helpful when you're trying to manoeuvre it around curved edges or into grooves to smooth them off.

Watch Out!

Before you take off the cupboard doors, have a pot or box at the ready. Store all the hinges, handles and relevant screws in it while you paint the doors – you don't want to be putting everything back together and find you've mislaid a crucial screw!

If you're replacing the cupboard handles as well as painting the doors, check the screw holes for the handles before you repaint. If they're larger than the existing ones, you might need to plug them with filler before you paint.

Make sure your freshly painted doors are completely dry and no longer tacky before you screw on any handles or put them back on your cabinets. This will reduce the risk of any chips or smudges ruining your new finish.

> Changing Handles

Cabinet hardware might sound dull; however, it's really anything but – it's an easy and inexpensive way to update your kitchen units and give them a whole new look. It can be a stand-alone project focusing on existing doors, or the finishing touch to newly painted doors and drawers. With just a few handles you can shift your style from traditional to modern, or from nondescript to country-kitchen or designer. Whatever you choose, it's a great opportunity to get the style and statement that you want.

Although cabinet hardware isn't necessarily the central focus of your kitchen, in the way that the fridge or the hob might be, it's always on display. It also plays a very practical role given how frequently it's used. It must therefore be fitted properly, hardwearing enough to withstand daily use, and look good. In the pages that follow, we'll take you through how to install and replace cabinet hardware efficiently and effectively.

YOU WILL NEED

- **Screwdriver**
- **Wood putty – in the correct shade for your cabinet doors and drawers, or a few shades to mix together**
- **Putty knife**
- **Clean damp cloth**
- **Hardware installation jig – an adjustable tool designed to allow accurate drilling of cabinet handle and knob holes**
- **Your chosen kitchen hardware**
- **Pencil**
- **Drill and drill bit suitable for the screws you're using**
- **Screws**

HOW TO

1 Remove any existing hardware by loosening the screws on the back of the cabinet doors or drawers. If your new hardware needs affixing in a different position, use the wood putty (ideally in a good shade match for your cabinets if you're not repainting them) to fill in the old

screw holes. Sometimes you might need to mix together two or three shades of putty to achieve the correct colour. Use your finger to apply the putty, then push enough in so that the hole is filled completely.

2 Use the putty knife to compact the putty, then draw the blade across the hole to create a smooth surface. Wipe the clean damp cloth around the hole to remove any excess. Let the putty dry completely before continuing.

3 Use the hardware installation jig and a pencil to create screw-hole markings that match your new handles.

4 Select a drill bit that corresponds with the size of your new handles' screws, then carefully drill where the pencil markings are, using steady and even pressure (see Toni's Top Tip on page 120).

5 It's time to attach your new handles. Line them up with the holes you've just drilled and secure in place with the screws, tightening with a screwdriver, if necessary. Repeat these steps across all your cabinets then step back and admire your lovely new kitchen units!

Toni's Top Tip

For loose screws in cupboard-door handles or in the fixtures to any other wooden surfaces, push one or more cocktail-/matchsticks into the hole and break off flush before putting the screws back in.

Toni's Top Tip

If this is your first time using a hardware installation jig, or replacing cabinet handles, try drilling a few practice holes into some scrap wood.

If you're doing a complete unit makeover and painting your drawers and cupboard doors too, remove the handles, fill in any holes that are no longer needed, and drill new holes for the new hardware before you start painting. This will give you a slicker look.

> Kitchen Splashbacks

Splashbacks, whether they're behind the hob only or along the full length of the countertops, give a great opportunity to make a statement and inject some colour and personality into your space. They've moved on in recent years from being a practical feature to keep your walls clean and dry to a more aesthetic consideration. They're also a part of the kitchen that is easy to update and changing them can be done independently of the rest of the kitchen furniture.

Materials suitable for use as splashbacks range from toughened glass, acrylic and stainless steel, to natural stone and tiles. Tiles can be whatever shape, style, colour and pattern you like, and can be a very personal statement. Glass is easy to clean and reflects light well, and, because it comes in a rainbow of colours, can offer a real contrast to units or neutral wall colours. If you want to use bricks, make sure they are sealed, to protect them against grease and water damage.

Watch Out!

Don't use laminate splashbacks behind a gas hob or an oven – their plastic quality means they shouldn't be exposed to open flames or direct heat.

Personalize your splashback

Members of the DIY OAB group have come up with some really ingenious and personal ways to create great-looking statement splashbacks that are also practical and inexpensive. Consider some of these:

- For a really unique look and personal touch, there are companies that will create splashbacks from your favourite poster, artwork or even photographs of your family. Have a look on the DIY OAB group for ideas or search online.

- A cheap solution to damaged tiles (or tiles that you just don't like the colour or look of) is to cover them with tile stickers, which are readily available online in a wide variety of styles and patterns. All you have to do is peel off the backing paper and stick onto clean, dry tiles.

- Use your favourite beer mats, playing cards, old corks, pebbles or pennies as a splashback. You can do this with anything you like, but remember to seal in your style.

- A blackboard can be a really fun and useful splashback – perfect for writing down shopping lists; just paint a kitchen wall with chalkboard paint (see page 184) – although it's best to do this away from the hob to avoid grease spatter.

Watch Out!

If you're using superglue or a silicone adhesive to fix anything to the walls in a kitchen, make sure it's heatproof and/or waterproof.

> Kitchen Counters

These much-used work surfaces are one of the most commonly cited elements of the home that the DIY OAB community wishes they could change. Whether you've moved into a new place or are simply tired of looking at your scratched, chipped, dented and worn-out counters, it's easy to understand why they're such a cause of grievance. They're just so *visible*, but what can you do with them?

While most of us aren't quite ready to have some lovely new stone work surfaces fitted – nor can we afford them! – there are lots of inexpensive ways to give your kitchen counters a boost. Have a look through these simple ideas for a new style, for inspiration and to help you get to get to grips with the different options out there.

Paint

Yes, that's right, you can paint your worktops! This idea works best with wooden surfaces but you can paint laminate counters, too – you'll just have to prep them a little more beforehand. This means sanding them, priming them and then applying two, maybe three, coats of paint. As with any surface, make sure you use an appropriate hardwearing paint, and always remember to seal it with wax, varnish or resin, as recommended by the paint manufacturer. It takes some work but is far cheaper than buying brand new tops!

Fresh varnish

Of course, this is only really appropriate for wooden worktops, but a new coat of varnish can give even the most tired surfaces a fresh glow. If you like, you can go a bit darker with the shade, or, if you don't mind putting in the time for some sanding, you could finish them in a lighter colour.

Bring back vinyl

If you love the idea of stone but don't love the price tag, you can get a really good copy of the look using self-adhesive vinyl. There's such a wide range of vinyl colours and styles out there, and it's an affordable and durable material. It definitely takes a bit of skill to apply it correctly to your worktops (and to do so wrinkle free – see page 114), so it's best to have a second pair of hands to help you. As ever, make sure you prep your surface thoroughly beforehand and feel confident about what you're doing – read those instructions on the packaging carefully!

Try tiles

Too much texture on a kitchen surface might be a big no-go for some people – after all, crevices where food might get stuck or forgotten about isn't ideal, and grouting can be a real hotspot for that. However, a tiled worktop can look really contemporary and allow you to inject a solid dose of personal style and self-expression. There's a host of budget-friendly self-adhesive tile sheets now available, too, so it might be an even easier and cheaper project than you think.

Overlay overlay

You can buy very thin slabs of material, such as stone, that can be fitted over the top of your current worktops. It's a much more cost-efficient option than replacing them with full stone tops, and gives you a lovely finish and a great look.

New laminate

There's a reason why the vast majority of households have laminate worktops – they're inexpensive, easy to keep clean and hardwearing. So, why not think about an upgrade? If your kitchen is getting on a bit, you might be surprised at the quality of some of the newer ranges of laminate tops, so it's well worth look into replacing your existing ones. It will instantly make the kitchen look fresh and clean.

Toni's Top Tip

Use sealant around your sink to stop water from getting under your vinyl worktops and to avoid them peeling off.

> Hidden Storage

There never really seems to be enough space in the kitchen for all your stuff, whether that's food, cutlery, crockery, pans or appliances, or the other paraphernalia that creeps into most family hubs on a day-to-day basis. If you often find yourself thinking, 'Well, where am I going to put it?!', this section is for you.

Figuring out smart and hidden storage solutions for the kitchen can be a real challenge, especially if you have a big family. If you're sick of tripping over toys, jamming food into overstuffed cupboards or opening a drawer and causing a Tupperware avalanche, read on for some great ideas for hidden storage.

Pull-out vertical shelving

Perfect for kitchen spaces, these vertically stacked larder-type drawers take up little space and make otherwise hard-to-store items easily accessible. The pull-out mechanism makes them effortlessly smooth to use, too. If height is an issue, you might want to buy some kitchen steps to reach the top shelves, or fill those spaces with items that are used less often.

The gaps

The gap between your ceiling and your tallest cupboards or bookshelves is usually underutilized because it isn't at eye level or requires a little effort to reach it. However, again, this is where a set of humble kitchen steps can help you to make use of every hidden corner of your home. By simply placing some boxes or baskets up there, you've created another smart and tidy-looking storage area for those appliances or other items you only occasionally use.

Above windows

This tip for yet another underrated gap works well not only in kitchens but also in dining rooms and living rooms. Fit a shelf above your window and you've created a space where you can place decorative but practical boxes and baskets, or display some of your favourite space-takers, such as vases and items of kitchenware.

Hanging out

This isn't just a storage tip, it can also look really stylish . . . Hang your nicest chopping boards or pans from the wall. Source some reclaimed wood, attach a row of cute hooks to it, fix it to your wall and you have the perfect hanging rack. You'll now have everything visible and to hand, and will likely free up a whole drawer's worth of space in the process.

Kitchen island

If you have a kitchen island with space underneath it, use some or all of it for storage by fitting it with some shelves or drawers. You'll be surprised how large this space actually is and you'll be able to squeeze in all those extra bits and pieces that clutter your worktops.

Splashback shelves

Your splashback is another area of the kitchen that sits mostly empty, so why not fit some shelves to it? Don't place them too low, though, otherwise whatever you put on them might end up getting spattered with food and grease. Note that it's only really possible to do this on tiles or plaster – don't try it with glass!

Mirror or cupboard?

This is a larger DIY project but really worth it, as the end result is both functional and fun. Fit a full-length mirror as a door to a built-in cupboard with shelves. The mirror will add light to a dark space and make a small kitchen look bigger. This idea can work well in bedrooms or even bathrooms, too, to store your clothes, skincare or even towels.

Dining Areas

Most of us don't have the luxury of a separate dining room. Quite often, even if space in a house allows for one, it gets turned into a playroom, another living room or even a bedroom, as all of these options will get more use than a formal dining room. However, dining spaces are important for families, as they offer an opportunity for everyone to sit around a table and share news from their day.

Don't worry if your home is too small to accommodate a whole dining room; anyone can create a corner that will provide a place for a table, a few chairs and a chance to come together.

Tips for doubling up your dining space

- Buy an extendable table and keep it as small as it needs to be for day-to-day use. If you're entertaining a few extra guests, simply make the table bigger then return it to its more compact size afterwards.

- If your dining area is part of a bigger room, add a rug under the table or hang a pendant light overhead to give the illusion of a separate, dedicated area.

- If your kitchen-diner-lounge is an open-plan space and you don't want to be looking at the table all the time, position it behind the sofa. This divides the space and marks it out as a separate 'room'.

> Breakfast Bars and Kitchen Islands

If you don't have the space for a permanent dining table, a breakfast bar can be a great addition to sit at for a chat and a cup of tea, or to eat meals. It's a great space-saving option as it can be positioned against a wall or incorporated into a kitchen island, which can double up as a storage unit.

The standard height for a breakfast bar is 90cm, but if it's raised above the worktop it should be 1.2m. In this case, to sit at it comfortably, go for height-adjustable stools with footrests as your seating option.

If you decide on a kitchen island, make sure that the countertop overhangs by at least 30cm, so you can get a stool/your legs underneath it comfortably. Remember that you'll also need to allow for another 60cm of space behind your seats, for access.

Homemade kitchen island

As well as being a really useful storage and eating feature, an island is a great, informal dining option for an existing kitchen. Keep your space relaxed and inviting with this brilliantly versatile and easy-to-make DIY project.

ALLOW TIME FOR . . .

- **The adhesive to bond and dry**

YOU WILL NEED

- Wooden box or cupboard unit to your required size
- MDF sheet(s) to fit to the top of the unit with overhang to allow for stools
- Pencil and tape measure
- Strong wood glue
- Drill and screws (optional)
- Vinyl wrapping sheets

HOW TO

1   For this easy kitchen island you need a wooden box or cupboard unit. The size you go for will depend on your height and how much space you have in the kitchen. You can pick one up from any homeware or DIY store.

2   You'll also need to fit a work surface on top of it. You can buy a proper kitchen worktop to match the existing ones in your kitchen, or you can buy a thick piece of MDF and cover it with vinyl or paint it. If you want to be able to sit at it, make sure that you have a 30cm overhang on one side of it.

3   Set the MDF on the floor and place the unit on top of it, upside down, to get the position right. Use a measuring tape to check it's sitting centrally with equal borders around it, apart from the 30cm overhang on one side. Once you're happy with the position, draw a pencil outline of the box on the MDF. Move the box to one side and squiggle some strong wood glue on the MDF, within the outline of the box shape where the top of the unit will

go. Then, lower the unit back in place and leave it to set, according to the glue manufacturer's guidelines.

4   Once dry, flip the unit over. If it doesn't feel solid enough, drill some holes in the four corners and secure the MDF top to the unit with screws.

5   Finally, wrap the top and outer, visible edges of the MDF with some vinyl sheeting to give it a worktop look and make it waterproof (see page 114 for advice on wrapping).

Toni's Top Tip

If you like, you can attach lockable castors to the bottom of the unit and create a moveable island that you can shift to the side of the room when you need more space. Simply fix a wheel to each corner of the unit. If it's a large unit, add some central castors, too.

Kitchen-Diner-Lounge

Toni's Choice

The kitchen is the heart of every home and I've chosen Joanne Stichcombe's kitchen to feature as the group project for this chapter. She's used so many of the elements we at DIY OAB rely on to create her dream kitchen for her extended family – from repainting store-bought cabinets to making her own table and stools; from sourcing second-hand furniture to repurposing scaffolding boards as shelves. Joanne makes use of most of the tips and tricks in this book, so I won't list the how-tos again here; instead, let her description inspire you to flip through these pages to create your own ideal kitchen. To quote Joanne: 'I don't particularly follow any designers, I just like what I like.' Hear, hear, Joanne!

Member's Method

My name's Joanne and I'm a very keen DIY decor designer. My husband Simon and I gained our DIY skills over years of practice as we renovated each of our properties to the best of our ability, using online videos when we needed to. We had struggles along the way with plumbing, electrics and gas works, which we always leave to the professionals.

I'm inspired by interior design books and magazines, and the odd TV programme. I take bits from here and there, put it all together in my head and strive to create the look I've imagined. I really enjoy coming up with designs then bringing them to life. I also like making my own furniture as well as finding bargains online and at the cheaper discount stores. My favourite part is dressing the rooms once they're complete.

This kitchen is my favourite room as I've put my heart and soul into making a large open-plan kitchen-diner-lounge with bifold doors to give an outside–inside feel where I can enjoy cooking with the family. I love the New York loft look, which is what inspired me with this kitchen project. We wanted a rustic feel, so we used ceramic brick-effect wall tiles and ceramic oak-effect floor tiles. The whole kitchen was designed around the central island which serves as a gathering point for our large family. The kitchen itself was a basic white kitchen from a big-box furniture retailer, which we fitted ourselves. We painted the doors and drawers in four coats of our choice of colour, finished off with a top coat. We bought solid-oak worktops from the same retailer. We wanted a big island so all the grandchildren can sit around it when they come to visit. The sideboard was a second-hand bargain. We made the coffee table, stools and shelving from recycled scaffolding boards, which we sanded and stained to carry through the rustic look. We made the lights from cheap spider pendants purchased online and some wood from pallets which we stained and sanded down.

My advice to other DIY OABers would be that, if you like a certain design or designs, you can mix and match items – they don't all have to be in one style. I don't particularly follow any designers, I just like what I like.

Watch Out!

The kitchen is full of electrical and plumbing jobs – don't try doing these yourself. This is the time to hire a professional.

Members' Top Tips

- If you can't imagine the design in your head, use a room design app. There are many free ones available from the various app stores.

- As Joanne says, things don't always have to match, so try scouring your local charity shops and freebie sites for furniture and accessories!

Members' Comments

😍 👏 🖤 🔥 Love the blue cupboards and brickwork . . .
Stunning home. *Amanda Marsh*

This is my idea of heaven! I love this! *Maxi Morris*

I really like this. Beautiful kitchen. *Linda Ann*

Wonderful! I love your floor plan – how nice to be able to
work in the kitchen and visit with others. *Vivianna Mason*

Budget and Schedule Planner

Vision: What do you want to achieve?

Start with the end product so you have a clear idea of where you are going. Pictures, sketches and mood boards can help here, and you can refer back to them as you progress and/or use them for motivation.

My Vision

....

....

....

....

....

....

....

....

....

Budget

Once you've costed everything you need, start looking for savings wherever possible using the 7 Golden Rules on page 8, including borrowing, reusing, deal-hunting and hiring equipment.

Use the table below to work out your budget.

WHAT YOU NEED	Cost	GOLDEN RULE SAVING OPTION	Savings
	£		£
	£		£
	£		£
	£		£
	£		£
	£		£
	£		£
	£		£
	£		£
TOTAL COST £		TOTAL SAVINGS £	

Total cost – total savings = budget £

Overspend contingency of 10% £

Total £

Schedule

Breaking down your project into tasks and steps can help make larger projects more manageable and less daunting, and can give you a clear path to achieving your goal. If you're short on funds, you can also plan to get to a point where you can enjoy your progress to date while you save towards doing more.

TASKS/STEPS	TARGET COMPLETION DATE
1	
2	
3	
4	
5	
6	
7	
8	
9	
10	

The Living Room

The living room (or sitting room, lounge, front room, family room – whatever you call it!) is one of the most important rooms in the house. It's where you unwind after a rubbish day or snuggle up with your partner or the kids. It's where you have a giggle with your friends or make small talk with the in-laws. Whether you're a comfy-cosy kinda person or the queen of modern and clutter free, it's worth spending a bit of extra time and effort to make this space yours.

One thing that's worth bearing in mind is how often you like to revamp your decor. If you're always lusting after new trends, try to keep the bones of your living room fairly neutral – think white or grey walls. There are loads of accessories that you can mix and match – from stick-on mirrors to temporary shelving – to update your home without having to get into major renovations or expense. So if you love a style reset, remember to save bold colours for your accessories.

This section is full of ideas for jobs – big and small – that you can do yourself to freshen up your living room easily and inexpensively. From great fakes, such as creating a functioning fireplace, to fashioning a focal point and hanging curtains and pictures, these ideas will give your living room a much-needed lift.

> <u>Dyeing Sofas, Carpets and Rugs</u>

Sometimes a beloved piece of furniture can start to look a bit worn, or perhaps you've been given a chair, rug or carpet, or bought one second-hand and it needs a bit of TLC. Maybe the colour no longer suits the room, or it's simply faded and uneven in shade? Don't chuck it out, because there's a simple way to refresh your furnishings. Fabric-dyeing can give an item a new lease of life, whether you're going for a subtle change or a total transformation.

ALLOW TIME FOR . . .

- **The fabric to dry overnight – allow time for drying if steam-cleaning, too**

WHAT YOU NEED

- **Dust sheets**
- **Warm water (quantity depends on size of item)**
- **Dye (quantity and type depends on item size and fabric – see Toni's Top Tip on page 144)**
- **Spray bottle (wide and fine spray)**
- **Rubber gloves**
- **Medium-bristle scrubbing brush and bucket or bathtub (depending on size of item)**

HOW TO

1 Start by cleaning the item thoroughly; rugs and sofas can be vacuumed but it's best to steam-clean carpets – if you don't have a steam-cleaner, you can hire one for the day and do all your other carpets too!

2 Check the sort of fabric you will be dyeing, as this can affect what type of dye you need and how well it will take.

3 If you're dyeing furnishings and rugs indoors, lay out dust sheets underneath them; if possible, dye larger items like sofas outside.

4 Mix the dye and warm water in the spray bottle following the instructions on the dye packaging. It might take a few attempts to get the ratio right, but starting with one part dye to three parts water is a good rule of thumb.

5 Put on your gloves then spot-test a small area of fabric with the dye solution and leave to dry.

6 For fitted carpets, remove all furniture from the room, and spray the carpets with dye solution only once they're fully dried from the steam clean. If you're happy with the spot-test, spray the whole item with the liquid, making sure to soak it evenly, then gently rub the liquid into the fibres with a brush. Smaller rugs can be submerged in a large bucket or bathtub filled with your dye solution, if preferred.

Toni's Top Tip

The easiest fabrics for DIY dyeing are chenille, velvet, wool, polyester and cotton. When dyeing carpets and rugs, don't use machine/submersion dyes as these are not colourfast. Instead, use an all-in-one liquid fabric dye.

7 If you've dyed a rug by submerging it, transfer it to your washing machine and wash with gentle laundry detergent and warm water, then remove and dry it flat on top of a dust sheet laid out on the floor.

8 To avoid colour transfer, allow the sofa, rug or carpet to dry completely before using. Once dry, if the colour isn't as strong as you want it to be, repeat the process with another application.

Watch Out!

Spot-testing in an inconspicuous area on your item or carpet is the best way to avoid disappointment in the colour – or, worse, disaster by damage!

> Feature Walls

Feature walls are interior or exterior walls that are distinctly different from the rest of the room through colour, shade, design or materials. Bright and colourful feature walls are increasingly popular in living rooms, bedrooms, and even kitchens. They're an exciting and inexpensive way to add extra style to a room, breathe new life into it and completely change the sense of the space, without having to totally redecorate.

You can create this look in a lot of different ways – from going dark and chic to introducing vibrant patterns – always tapping into your own personal style. That being said, if you need a bit of inspiration and guidance, here's your one-stop guide to what to avoid, points to remember, and how to decide on the approach you're going to take.

Do . . .

- Choose the right wall – take your time deciding which one you want to bring to life (see the Which Wall? box on page 147 for tips).

- Look around for inspiration – search online groups and resources, such as DIY OAB or Pinterest, for examples of feature walls with the colour or style you have in mind. It might confirm your vision or totally change your plans!

- Think about shape – consider the other walls in the room and how the feature will affect the look of those. There are several apps available that allow you to take a picture of your space to visualize what a feature wall would look like within it.

- Think about the room and the kind of mood you want to achieve, then decide on the colour/texture/pattern you want to go for.

- Sleep on your chosen colour/style – darker shades in a lighter room generally work best for feature walls, but lighter options can still look great. Over-coordinating a room with colours can often be too much, so whatever your choice, sleep on the decision and come back to it. Do you still love it?

- Trust yourself – the beauty of a feature wall is that it doesn't take for ever to do. Worst-case scenario – if you don't like it, you can always change it.

Don't . . .

- Be afraid to go bold – feature walls in neutral rooms really help to add colour. Subtle shades can look great, but perhaps experiment with something daring.

- Be restrained by walls – we've seen a growth in colour-blocking features on the DIY OAB group, with members painting one area of a wall, or a unique shape on it. We've also seen members paint the corner of a room, a box on multiple walls or the ceiling, and sometimes even doors.

- Forget about textures – if you want to liven up the room and draw focus, use tiles, wood panelling (see page 42) or wallpaper to add flair.

- Buy too much paint – follow the manufacturer's advice on paint coverage. You don't want to end up spending more money than you need to on paint you'll likely only use once.

Which wall?

It's important to get your focal point right; it is not always the wall you see when you first walk into a room. Instead, choose the wall you want to draw attention to because it's interesting or unique in some way, such as the one behind the bed headboard, or a wall on which you have a TV or large mirror. Similarly, walls with architectural interest, such as the chimney breast around a fireplace, or an alcove, can help to add another dimension to the feature.

How to make that feature wall pop

The key here is to get the style just right. What are you going for – subtle and elegant, or loud and dramatic? Here are some tips on choosing a style to fit your room and the mood you're after:

- Geometric paint or wallpaper is bold in a bedroom or can liven up a living room.

- A neutral tone, such as a subtle taupe, sand or olive shade, will bring a sense of calm and elegance to a room.

- A stone-effect accent, such as brickwork or masonry wallpaper, can bring an industrial vibe to a living room or kitchen. You can also go one step closer to the real thing and apply faux stonework (see page 151).

- Vertical rainbow stripes are great fun for a child's bedroom, as is a chalkboard wall.

- Black looks stylish in bathrooms, especially when paired with matching silver or chrome hardware.

- Headboard wall panelling can bring a hotel feel to your bedroom (see page 230).

- Botanical prints are lovely if you are a maximalist who loves colour, and a wallpapered wall with a strong print is the perfect way to make things more vibrant.

- Two-tone painting can produce a horizontal band of colour that creates a sense of height in a room. A particularly great colour for this idea is a muted green tone with a lighter shade on top.

Toni's Top Tip

Get yourself some tester pots and paint a small swatch on the wall, just as you would if you were considering painting the whole room. Alternatively, paint a piece of cardboard and prop it up against the wall to test the look of the colour in the room.

> Fireplaces

If you're lucky enough to have a fireplace, you'll know how cosy and comforting one can be. There's something appealing about a stylish fire surround, whether it's a fire crackling away at Christmas or the mantelpiece serving as a place to display some candles and family photographs for the rest of the year – not to mention how it can really pull a room together as an interesting focal point. If you have a fireplace already and you're looking to give it a makeover on a budget, there are a number of options to choose from, depending on your personal style.

Painting the surround (stone or brick)

Before you begin, there are a few things you need to consider: if your fireplace is functional, you must use heat-resistant paint to withstand the temperatures it will reach when in use. However, if it's purely decorative, it's OK to just use standard interior paint. If you're looking to reinvigorate a marble fire surround, it's best to sand the entire unit before you apply primer, followed by a latex-based or chalk paint in a single flat colour.

ALLOW TIME FOR . . .

- **Overnight drying after cleaning, plus paint drying**

WHAT YOU NEED

- Dust sheets
- Painter's tape
- Wire scrubbing brush
- Rubber gloves
- Clean damp cloth
- A few drops of washing-up liquid or vinegar
- Paint roller (suitable for textured surfaces)
- Primer (stain blocking, oil-based three-in-one – primer, sealant and undercoat)
- Oil-based paint
- Small paint brush

HOW TO

1   As always, cover up and protect the surrounding area, and make sure your dust sheet is taped down securely. If relevant, mark the edges of the area you want to paint with painter's tape.

2   Clean your fire surround. Whatever it is you plan to do, use a wire scrubbing brush to get rid of any dust, ash or cobwebs, then wipe down with a clean cloth dampened with water and a drop of washing-up liquid, or water and a few drops of vinegar. Leave to dry overnight.

3   Use a roller to apply a coat of primer to protect against future soot or scorch marks. Use your paint brush to reach any tricky spots.

4   Apply a second coat of primer and allow to dry.

5   Once the primer is dry, apply your chosen paint using the roller, and again, touch up any hard-to-reach areas with the paint brush.

Toni's Top Tip

Fireplaces are often associated with more traditional decor, but if you love a contemporary look, painting your fire surround a bold, eye-catching colour can create a gorgeous focal point for your space.

Faux natural stone

Rustic stone fireplaces are perfect for those who love a country-cottage vibe, but using traditional stone to achieve the look could end up breaking the bank. That's where heat-resistant stone-wall cladding for fireplaces comes in – it withstands extreme temperatures, looks and feels like real stone, and is really affordable. So if you're looking to bring a bit of traditional warmth to your fireplace, stone-wall cladding could be the solution.

ALLOW TIME FOR . . .

- **The stone-wall cladding to acclimatize – 24 hours**
- **Overnight drying for the adhesive**

WHAT YOU NEED

- **Heat-resistant stone-wall cladding for fireplaces**
- **Clean damp cloth**
- **Power mitre saw**
- **Protective gloves and goggles**
- **Specialist adhesive (ask for guidance from a member of staff when purchasing the cladding in store)**
- **Putty knife**

HOW TO

1   Allow the stone-wall cladding time to acclimatize by removing it from its packaging. As you do this, scrape off any stray bumps left over from the factory-moulding process. Leave in the room for 24 hours.

2   As always, clean the area where you will be placing the fireplace surround and allow it to dry.

3   Stack your stones until you find a configuration you're happy with – for a natural look, mix up the different shades of cladding and make sure the edges do not align perfectly (if they do, trim the relevant blocks with your power saw, wearing gloves and goggles).

4   Once you're happy with your design, you can start fixing the stones.

5   If this is a wall installation, start at the bottom and work your way up horizontally. However, if you're working with

a real fireplace, start at the top row and work outwards, as the top row is most visible and you'll want to achieve the most seamless look.

6 In order to attach the stones, apply a thick layer of adhesive to the back of each block and press it firmly to the wall surface. Use a clean damp cloth to remove any stray adhesive from the surface of the blocks.

7 If you're covering a real fireplace, you'll need to do the inside too. Fit the supplied corner blocks first, then add the rest of your blocks around these.

8 If any of the stones slip, especially on the top row, simply push them back up and, if necessary, use a piece of plasterboard or similar to prop up the bricks as they dry.

9 Allow the stones to dry on the wall, then step back and admire your stone-effect fireplace!

Wallpapered chimney breast

A chimney breast provides the ideal opportunity to create a bold statement or tie together a whole room's decor. One of my favourite ideas, and a very popular option, is applying brick-effect wallpaper, which creates an amazing optical illusion that can totally change the look of a room.

ALLOW TIME FOR . . .

- **Wallpaper paste drying**
- **Overnight drying after cleaning**

WHAT YOU NEED

- **Dust sheets**
- **Stepladder**
- **Fine-grit (120) sandpaper**
- **Clean damp cloth**
- **Sugar soap**
- **Tape measure**
- **Chalk or pencil**
- **Wallpaper of your choice (we love a whitewashed brick effect)**
- **Plumb line**
- **Wallpaper scissors or Stanley knife**
- **Wallpaper paste**
- **Pasting roller**
- **Pasting brush and paper-hanging brush**

HOW TO

1 Cover the surrounding area with dust sheets and tape them down to prevent a trip hazard. Remove any old wallpaper and lining paper (see Toni's Top Tip opposite) and sand down the wall, if necessary, for a smooth finish.

2 Clean the wall by wiping it down with a clean damp cloth and some sugar soap, and allow to dry overnight.

3 Use your tape measure to work out the width of your chimney breast. From there, find and mark the central point with some chalk or a pencil.

> ## Toni's Top Tip
>
> *When trying to remove stubborn lining paper, mix a capful of fabric conditioner in a washing-up bowl of warm water. Use a roller to 'paint' the wall with the solution and leave for 2 minutes, after which time it should come away much more easily.*

4 Next, measure half the width of your wallpaper roll and, using your plumb line, chalk a vertical line to indicate this distance from the left of the centre point. This is the 'plumb' that will be used as a reference for hanging the wallpaper.

5 Again, use your tape measure to record the distance from the ceiling to the mantel shelf, then from the ceiling to the floor. When you come to use these measurements to cut the wallpaper, allow around 10cm extra for each, to provide space for trimming.

6 In order to centre the design (not the seam), your first length of wallpaper (cut for ceiling-to-mantel measurement) should be hung to the left of the 'plumb'. Apply the paste to the wall using a roller and make sure you include a few centimetres either side of the area where you're adding your first length, to make sure the edges stick securely.

7 Ensuring the paper is centred with its edge flush to the left side of the chalked plumb, use your wallpaper brush to flatten the length to the wall, brushing the paper down and out.

8 Once you're happy with it, use the back of your scissors to mark where you need to trim excess paper at the top and bottom. Ease the paper away from the wall, trim, then ease back into place.

9 Repeat the process with the next length(s), moving out from the plumb to cover the right-hand side of the chimney breast, and using the longer (ceiling-to-floor) pieces to cover the breast areas at either side of the mantel.

10 To paper the corners of the chimney breast, start at the corner away from the wall and apply the paper back into the recess.

Toni's Top Tip

Love the look of a traditional hearth or woodburner but don't have the space or cash to get one installed? The DIY OAB members have just the solution – fake it till you make it! You can buy very affordable electric stoves online, and freestanding fire surrounds at most DIY outlets. Add a brick-effect wallpaper background and a faux hearth, and you've got a gorgeous fireplace, without the hassle or expense of a large-scale renovation.

> <u>Window Dressing</u>

Dressing windows is a detail that's often left until last, but this finishing touch deserves your attention. Many windows are a focal point in a room, so dressing them well will really frame your space. On the other hand, some are pretty functional-looking and might benefit from slatted blinds or shutters instead.

Before getting started, familiarize yourself with the different options – drapes that hang from the curtain pole right to the floor; curtains that are just the length of the window; shades, blinds or continental shutters. Consider the aesthetics of the window – do you want to highlight it or disguise it? Also, think about the practicalities – if the room is dark, you might want to choose window coverings that allow in the maximum amount of light during the day, or you might want to install blackout blinds to make the room as dark as possible.

There's a style to suit every budget, interior and practical purpose, so be sure to consider your choices carefully and shop around to get exactly what you need.

Drill down to the details

Got the practicalities sorted and know the sort of covering you want? Here are a few ideas to get you started on the design details to personalize the look for your home.

- Love a statement? Look for bold patterned curtains, or introduce a strong single colour and texture with your fabrics around the window, finishing them off with decorative ties.

- To add height to a room, go for floor-to-ceiling curtains in a light fabric and neutral colour.

- A 'café curtain', otherwise known as a half curtain, will suit a smaller window that doesn't have a view beyond it, and is practical and pretty.

- Create an attention-grabbing bay window by combining blinds and long drapes that follow the curve of the bay.

- Shutters don't have to be painted plain white – for a dramatic effect try navy, or even black.

- Make a narrow or small window feel bigger by choosing a curtain pole that's wider than the window and fix it slightly higher than the window frame. A clever illusion!

- Consider the external view – what will your windows look like from the outside?

- Keep in mind what's right for your home. For example, longer curtains are more formal but can be less practical when it comes to furry friends and little ones. Keep in mind your style *and* your household.

Toni's Top Tips

If you want to hang a set of voile curtains behind your curtains, you don't have to replace your curtain pole with a double one. Simply run a bungee cord behind the length of the existing pole, then hang it on the final curtain hook at either end and pull it taut. Voilà – a second pole!

If you have eyelet curtains, cut some lengths of pipe lagging into 5cm pieces and slip these onto the curtain pole behind the curtain pleats to ensure even spacing. You can also use cut-up toilet-paper cardboard tubes to achieve the same look.

Don't be scared to ask for fabric swatches before you commit to ordering curtains or blinds – you'll feel more confident in your final decision if you can see these samples in place against the window and the other decor in your room.

Watch Out!

Take your measurements very carefully – mistakes can be costly and mean the window coverings look a mess if you end up patching or trimming to fit.

> Hanging Pictures

Hanging artwork and photographs is a lovely way to add a really personal touch to your house and make it feel like a home. A gallery wall – where lots of pictures are hung in a group – has become popular with members of the DIY OAB group. The added bonus is that once you've positioned the frames they can be easily updated with newer images as time goes on, without too much effort.

However, to get the maximum effect from pictures as a room feature, you need to hang them carefully. It isn't difficult, but it does mean a few considerations before you begin. So let's run through the key points for hanging pictures with pizazz.

What to consider

- What type of wall are you hanging the frames on? You'll more than likely be attaching them to plasterboard, but you'll need different fixings for brickwork or masonry.

- Are you happy putting fixings into the wall? For some renters, and even some homeowners, driving a nail or a fixing into a wall is a no-go. If this is the case, you might want to consider using the strong adhesive strips or other alternatives that are now available from most hardware shops, which will cause as little damage to the wall as possible, and many won't pull off paint when you remove them.

- How heavy is your frame or picture? Most small to midsize frames can be hung easily with standard fittings, but heavy frames will require more heavy-duty fixings, such as wall anchors, or will need to be fixed directly into wall studs.

- Don't forget about pipes and cables that might be running through the walls! You can use stud-checker sensors that detect woodwork, live wires or pipes. As a rule of thumb, wires generally run vertically around light switches and plug sockets, so avoid hammering in a direct line above or below these.

- What style is your frame? Frames have a variety of fixings on the back that can make your life easier – or harder! Some have picture wire running across the width or rectangular sawtooth hangers. Also, check whether your frame is indented; many IKEA frames have an inset lip, which means you'll need your fixing to protrude further from the wall than normal to ensure you can hang your picture on it properly and securely.

- Last but not least, where will your picture(s) go? Are you hanging a group of them or just one? Generally, you want to hang a picture roughly around eye level, although it is entirely up to you. If you want to hang multiple pictures, consider whether to go for a scattered, grouped or linear hanging style.

Toni's Top Tip

To see how a picture will look before you put it up, cut out a piece of paper or cardboard the size of your frame and stick it carefully to the wall with reusable blue or white putty tack or tape. This is also a really useful trick to do with multiple pictures/pieces of paper, to see how a grouping will look. Play around with different shapes and layouts before you commit, to find the style you love the most.

WHAT YOU NEED

- Stud finder
- Pencil
- Tape measure
- Fixings (whatever you are using)
- Hammer, drill or screwdriver
- Spirit level
- Ruler

HOW TO

1   Decide where you want to hang your picture(s). Hold the frame against the wall to find the right height and position or check out Toni's Top Tip above for a great trick to get the position spot on.

2   Determine what sort of wall you are hanging on. If it's not immediately obvious, give it a tap – plasterboard will sound slightly hollow, whereas masonry or woodwork will sound more solid. Use a stud finder to check for cables and pipes, or follow the advice on page 161 to make sure you've chosen a safe spot for your fixing.

3   Use a pencil to roughly mark the centre of the top of the frame on the wall.

4   Use a tape measure to measure the distance from the top of the frame to the fixing on the back. If it's being secured with picture wire, pull it taut, towards the top of the frame.

5   On the wall, draw a point at the same distance down from the mark you made at the top of the frame. Go up by a few millimetres, to ensure that the first spot will be covered by the frame, and mark the fixing point on the wall.

6   Attach your fixing to the wall on this mark – the size and weight of the frame will determine the type of fixing you need (see Which Fixtures and Fittings? overleaf).

7   Hang the picture on the fitting and use a spirit level to check it is straight at the top and hanging properly.

8   If you're hanging identical frames in a line, use a spirit level and ruler to make marks at the exact same height. If you are using different frames, repeat steps 3 and 4, using a spirit level to ensure the frames of the pictures are aligned, then measure the distance for the fitting on the new frame to ensure the tops of the frames hang square.

Toni's Top Tip

It can be really fiddly to get a picture hung with picture wire hooked onto the wall fixture, so try this simple hack. Slip the wire onto a fork, then use the fork to guide the string onto the nail or picture hook.

Which fixtures and fittings?

- Very small pictures can be hung from a nail driven straight into plasterboard, and most lightweight frames can be hung from a two-pin picture hook, providing the plaster is in good condition.

- Larger frames will need to be fixed directly into the wood of a stud in a wall frame using a screw, or cavity-wall anchor fixings suitable for plasterboard. To fit these, drill a corresponding hole into the plasterboard, hammer in the fixing, then insert a screw which will protrude from the fixing and allow you to hang your frame from it. Follow the same process for brickwork: drill an initial hole, then insert a rawl plug and screw into it.

- Adhesive strips allow you to attach something to a wall without having to make a hole. Check the manufacturer's guidelines for advice on what weight of frame the individual strips will hold, then follow the instructions for how to attach them to the frame and wall.

Watch Out!

Some adhesive strips can still leave marks on paintwork, which may require attention when you move out of a property. Test them in an inconspicuous area before committing to using them throughout a room.

Media Wall

Toni's Choice

Media walls are a huge trend in the DIY OAB group. They add that wow factor to a room and are not as costly as they look. However, they're not for beginner DIYers, as they involve building a stud wall, plasterboarding and plastering, so enlist some help for the tricky bits if you need to, and allow plenty of time for building, plaster drying and painting. I've chosen Lauren McLaughlin to share her experiences of her partner, Steven, building a media wall around an existing wall-mounted TV and fireplace. I think it looks like a million dollars and I'd love to chill out in her living room in front of the fire to watch TV!

Watch Out!

If you are fitting a fireplace into your media wall, make sure it has a front heater (it will be labelled as such), so that the heat doesn't get trapped in your wall recess. Also read the manufacturer's instructions about how much space should be allowed all around it, before you build your unit.

ALLOW TIME FOR . . .

- Plaster to dry
- Paint to dry

WHAT YOU NEED

- Tape measure and spirit level
- Wooden timbers
- Chop saw
- Protective gloves and goggles
- Nail gun
- Nails and screws
- Cordless drill
- Stanley knife
- Plasterboard
- Plaster
- Paint
- Decorator's caulk

HOW TO

1 Measure the dimensions of your TV and/or fireplace before you begin, taking into account any required clearance around either to prevent heat building up.

2 Mark the depth of your media wall on the floor and ceiling, ensuring you've left enough recessed space in your media wall for your TV or fireplace.

3 Plan the other storage elements you'd like to include in your media wall – for example, shelving for books, DVDs, CDs or records, and decorative items such as photos or artwork.

4 Run electrical wires from your TV to the wall socket if it is to be hidden by the stud wall of your media wall to hide unsightly wires and trip hazards. Always ensure you have access to the wall socket.

5 If you want to put lights in the shelving, plan and fit the wiring and any light fittings accordingly.

6 Build the stud wall frame using wooden timbers.

7 Fix the plasterboard to the stud wall frame, securing it with nails or a nail gun.

8 Mix the plaster according to the instructions on the packet. Plaster over the plasterboard to create a smooth finish. Allow the plaster to dry according to the instructions on the packet.

9 Use decorator's caulk to fill any spaces between the media wall and the wall or the floor.

10 Paint the plastered stud wall when dry with your chosen colour and finish.

11 Position and plug in your TV and add all other items to the shelves once the paint is dry.

Member's Method

Our television was already wall mounted, so my partner, Steven, built the media wall to surround it, incorporating both the TV and the fireplace. He found this a very straightforward process, first measuring the space, then cutting the wood to size and building the media wall gradually to fit the space around the TV and fireplace. Luckily, there were no disasters – it all went according to plan!

The media wall was part of the larger project of renovating our living/dining/kitchen area. We removed a wall to make a combined living/dining-room space and added the media wall in the living room to make the area feel more spacious. We had a joiner quote for the work initially, but due to the lockdown, Steven decided to give it a go as he had the time to do it. We're very glad we did it ourselves because it saved us money, gave us more floor space and looks great!

Members' Top Tips

- Make sure you have decorator's caulk to fill in any gaps.

- Your DIY store will cut the wood to size for you – for free!

- A chop saw or mitre saw is great for short, straight and angled cuts, while a circular saw is best for long straight cuts. A jigsaw is best for straight and curved cuts, but less accurate for angled cuts. You can rent these from tool-hire companies or borrow one from a friend or neighbour.

Members' Comments

That is absolutely stunning. *Christina Whitelaw*

Wow, awesome xxx *Kathleen 'Mammy' Hare*

OMG, I LOVE that! Could he come and build one
in my house?! *Natalie Gemma Smith*

Budget and Schedule Planner

Vision: What do you want to achieve?

Start with the end product so you have a clear idea of where you are going. Pictures, sketches and mood boards can help here, and you can refer back to them as you progress and/or use them for motivation.

My Vision

....

....

....

....

....

....

....

....

....

....

Budget

Once you've costed everything you need, start looking for savings wherever possible using the 7 Golden Rules on page 8, including borrowing, reusing, deal-hunting and hiring equipment.

Use the table below to work out your budget.

WHAT YOU NEED	Cost	GOLDEN RULE SAVING OPTION	Savings
	£		£
	£		£
	£		£
	£		£
	£		£
	£		£
	£		£
	£		£
	£		£
TOTAL COST £		TOTAL SAVINGS £	

Total cost − total savings = budget £

Overspend contingency of 10% £

Total £

Schedule

Breaking down your project into tasks and steps can help make larger projects more manageable and less daunting, and can give you a clear path to achieving your goal. If you're short on funds, you can also plan to get to a point where you can enjoy your progress to date while you save towards doing more.

TASKS/STEPS	TARGET COMPLETION DATE
1	
2	
3	
4	
5	
6	
7	
8	
9	
10	

Utility Rooms and Storage

For many of us who live in flats or small homes, the idea of a separate space for a utility room is something of a pipe dream, but for those who are lucky enough to have one (in one form or another), they are often the last place your mind goes to do a bit of DIY.

It's easy for our laundry spaces to become messy, unloved, and perhaps even a little bit damp, as functionality prevails over style. After all, they're a means to an end – simply the home of the washing machine where everyone chucks their dirty clothes. That doesn't have to be the case, though – the area can be a great candidate for adding more storage to accommodate the random stuff that clutters up our kitchens and hallways.

In this section we'll run through some of the top ways to take control of your laundry space on a small budget, and how to make that space work harder for your household. Don't worry if you don't have a utility space, this section is still for you, as the storage solutions and ways to maximize airing space can be applied to a spare room, a corner of the kitchen, a lean-to or a garage.

> Laundry Storage

More often than not, the utility room becomes a dumping ground for stuff that doesn't have a natural home anywhere else in the house – whether that's shoes, coats or general paraphernalia. However, with some careful planning you can turn it into an organized storage haven. Have a look at page 179 for storage ideas, too, as these can all be applied to utility items.

From cupboards to shelving units, boxes, bags and baskets, there are myriad ways to address the problems of the seemingly unavoidable floordrobe!

Laundry baskets

If your laundry system involves transporting washing from your machine to a drying rack or line outside, it helps to have a basket or two for this purpose. A great space-saving tip is to opt for collapsible baskets that can be stored away easily or hung on a wall.

Laundry cabinet

If you have the space, positioning a laundry cabinet near your washing machine will mean your dirty washing doesn't have to be on display. Consider a cabinet that has different sections, to separate your colours from your whites, or compartmentalize it using caddies. For those with less space, the most common option for storing dirty washing is a hamper, which can be made of plastic, fabric, or even wood. You can pick up budget-friendly ones in homeware stores or online.

Toni's Top Tip

Utility rooms are the perfect place to repurpose old kitchen units and use them for storage. So, for a cheap overhaul, check your local community groups to see if anyone is chucking some away (some kitchen shops will sell old showroom units cheaply too). If they don't look quite as you'd like, don't forget there are plenty of ways you can upcycle them to fit your style (see page 110).

> ### Toni's Top Tip
>
> *To prevent scuffs or tears in kitchen flooring when moving appliances, squirt a small amount of washing-up liquid or liquid soap on the floor beforehand, so that the appliance slides into place easily.*

> DIY Drying Rack

Whether you have a garden space or not, from time to time you'll need to hang clothes up to dry indoors, and it can feel like there is no perfect solution to the chaos this can create. Laundry day might often see clothes or sheets hung up on the backs of chairs and doors, or draped over the radiators. Surely there has to be a better way? Clothes airers are inexpensive and handy for indoor drying but are often clunky and awkward to store when not in use. So, read on for a host of DIY drying-rack options.

Wall-mounted wooden drying rack

Ready-made options can cost hundreds of pounds, but here's a way you can put together something that looks great, fits your style and is functional – for more like tens of pounds!

YOU WILL NEED

- 4 wooden struts to form the frame
- Jigsaw
- Screws and screwdriver
- Wooden dowels the length of your frame to be fitted within the frame
- Hinges and fastenings, or wall brackets

Toni's Top Tip

Go for a contemporary farmhouse look by upcycling an old wooden ladder to a hanging rack. Simply sand it down with fine-grit (120) sandpaper to smooth its surfaces, then seal and paint it with a moisture-resistant paint or varnish. Once dry, attach each end to the ceiling using ceiling hooks appropriate for your space. You can then hang clothes on it by draping them or using coat hangers. If you have a high ceiling, fit a pulley to it and tie a sturdy rope to each corner of the ladder that can be drawn up through the pulley for raising and lowering purposes.

HOW TO

1　Lay the four pieces of wood on the floor and build a rectangular wooden frame, screwing securely together with screws at each corner.

2   Position the wooden dowels to run along the interior span of the frame at an equal distance from one another, and screw in at each end of the frame. Use enough dowels to fit within the frame, leaving enough space between each dowel for your washing to dry.

3   The final step is to attach the rack to the wall using hinges and fastenings, or you can attach it to the wall using brackets that support the ends of the rectangle. Bear in mind that you will need wall fastenings that are strong enough to support the weight of the frame once it's loaded up with damp washing.

Toni's Top Tip

A simpler version of this wall dryer can be made by building a large wooden frame, with corner supports. Drill a series of holes in opposite ends of the frame at equal distances from one another, then secure lengths of clothes line across the frame instead of using dowels.

> Miscellaneous Storage

If you have a separate utility space or your laundry is in your kitchen, garage or otherwise, more storage is always going to be a bonus, be it a place to keep your washing powders and fabric conditioners, or somewhere for your baskets or cleaning products. There are so many great ideas out there to help you get organized for very little outlay.

Storage caddies

Open shelves can look messy, so consider buying some storage caddies to house everything. Practical, water-resistant plastic boxes will do the job nicely, or you can go for a more aesthetically pleasing look such as fabric or wicker. You can pick these up in supermarkets or bargain homeware stores for very little and you can even label them all. We'll leave that with you . . .

Upgrade your cupboards

Handy internal storage stackers can free up a surprising amount of space at the top of cupboards that often goes unused. Creating two tiers will often allow you to store more items, and you can also consider installing racks – for example upside-down spice racks – at the top of the cabinets to hang up cleaning products such as sprays. A series of hooks running down the inside of the cabinets also provides a place to hang any fiddly items.

Open stackable storage

Keep costs down by building up, with easy stackable storage. These modular designs are available at most homeware stores, but if you're feeling handy, you can also make your own out of MDF. Constructing units that extend up to ceiling height, and combining open cubes with caddies is a great way to maximize space. The beauty of this system is that you can add or take away units to suit your space.

Wall-mounted options

Floor storage is great but it does, of course, do one important thing – take up floor space! Adding shelves or storage units to your walls will maximize space without crowding your room, as will racks and hooks. You can buy budget shelves for next to nothing from DIY stores.

Think trolleys

A shelving unit on wheels might not seem like an obvious storage choice but, depending on its height, it can give you not only additional storage space, but also an additional worktop that can be moved around to suit your needs.

Toni's Top Tip

If you're tight on space in your utility room, try stacking your white goods. Tumble dryers can be housed above washing machines with the use of a stacking kit. Your washing machine can even go above an under-counter freezer or fridge. Two for one.

Watch Out!

If you're integrating appliances within cupboards, make sure the appliances are suitable for being housed this way, otherwise they can overheat and become a fire hazard.

> Chalkboard Wall

If you love to bring a bit of fun into your decor, chalkboard paint is a brilliant option. It's a great way to get creative with the kids, express your artistic side, or provide you with an opportunity to update your interior with just a few flicks of a chalk pen!

For many households, the utility room is where the freezer sits, and where cleaning products are stored, so what could be handier than a chalkboard wall where you can update your shopping list throughout the week?

This really playful idea can also work in the kitchen or the kids' playroom. It could even serve as a weekly planner to keep track of who is home and when!

ALLOW TIME FOR . . .

- Each coat of paint to dry – 1 hour
- The surface to fully dry before use – three days

WHAT YOU NEED

- Dust sheets
- Painter's tape
- Clean damp cloth
- Fine-grit (120) sandpaper
- Chalkboard paint
- Paint tray
- Foam roller
- Chalk sticks or pens
- Clean dry cloth

HOW TO

1   As with any painting project, use your dust sheets and painter's tape to ensure the area surrounding your workspace is protected from any splatters or drips.

2   Use the fine-grit (120) sandpaper to ensure the wall surface is even – chalkboard paint is thinner than regular indoor paint, so you need to remove any imperfections before you begin.

3   Wipe down the area to be painted with a clean damp cloth, carefully removing any dust as you go, and leave to dry.

4   Pour the paint into the tray.

5   Use the foam roller to begin painting. You want a light coat, so move the roller back and forth in the shallow end of the tray a few times to ensure it isn't dripping or overly heavy with paint.

6   Apply your paint to your chosen area, then leave it to dry for at least an hour before applying a second coat. Allow this one to dry for another hour before adding a third layer, if required.

7   Allow your new chalkboard to dry fully for a minimum of 24 hours, but ideally three days, before rubbing the entire painted area with the flat edge of a chalk stick to season it (also known as priming). Without this step, any marks you make on the chalkboard will leave 'ghosts' – meaning the marks will never erase completely. Once you've done that, rub the chalk into the wall using a clean dry cloth and it's ready for use.

Laundry Room

Toni's Choice

We don't all love sorting out our dirty laundry (or is that just me?!), but I was inspired by Amy Jane Shore's shabby-chic laundry room. She's created a cosy, stylish environment that makes the prospect of doing this less of a chore and more of a treat – nice one, Amy Jane!

WHAT YOU NEED

- Paint
- Spray paint
- Brushes for paint
- Shelves
- Sandpaper
- Brackets for shelves
- Screwdriver
- Screws
- Wallpaper
- Wallpaper paste
- Brushes for wallpaper paste
- Glass jars
- Lace or ribbon
- Faux (or real!) flowers

HOW TO

1 Paint any existing shelves in the colour of your choice.

2 If you need to install shelves first, try sourcing some second-hand ones or use pallet boards, which you can sand, paint, then install using brackets, screws and a screwdriver.

3 Mix the wallpaper paste according to the instructions on the packet, apply to the wallpaper and hang the wallpaper behind the shelves. (If you haven't yet installed the shelves, then I'd recommend hanging the wallpaper first, then fixing the shelves, as it can be a bit fiddly hanging wallpaper between shelves.)

4 Source a variety of glass jars from car-boot sales, second-hand shops or online retailers to store your cleaning products. You can also tie a length of ribbon or lace around them, and/or spray paint them in different colours, to use them to display your flower arrangements.

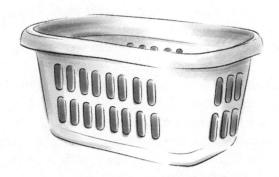

Member's Method

I decorated my laundry room during the lockdown and wanted a shabby-chic look that was in keeping with the rest of my house. I love the homely, floral, feminine look, and as the rest of my home is decorated in neutral colours, I decided that I'd use soft-pink accents to create a bright, pretty and cheerful room.

I wanted to have all my detergents and cleaning products to hand and display them on shelves in keeping with the look rather than have them hidden away in a cupboard. I bought some pink shelves and applied a little floral wallpaper to the back panels for a country-garden, shabby-chic touch. I filled the shelves with glass jars with a strip of lace or length of coloured satin ribbon tied around their necks.

I loved collecting pink accessories and buying pink and white laundry cleaners to keep with the colour scheme. I enjoyed decanting all the products into these glass jars so everything on view was in soft, clean shades. I even spray-painted a couple of Kilner jars in white and pink, and accessorized the shelves with fake flower heads and stems of flowers in jars to create a pretty, fresh feeling.

Most of the items were sourced cheaply – I used wooden crates from a pound store, and simple shelves that could be painted easily and had enough space for the jars. The washing basket was a charity-shop find that I painted a soft raspberry colour and embellished with coordinating florals.

My ultimate aim was to create a space with an old-fashioned laundrette feel that would make doing the laundry less of a chore. I chose washing machines with chrome door trims to tie in with the look and added a chandelier for a touch of elegance as well as a little table lamp with a pretty white lampshade for a subtler, more cosy light.

Watch Out!

Have a plumber install your washing machine to avoid any plumbing disasters.

Make sure cleaning products are kept in childproof containers and out of reach of any children that might visit your beautiful laundrette.

Members' Comments

This room makes me want to do laundry, which I despise but would gladly do all day just to hang out in this peaceful and lovely space . . . Great job. *Promise Banks*

Now, I don't normally like shabby chic, but my goodness, this is absolutely gorgeous! The most beautiful shabby chic I have ever seen. Amazing job, well done xx *Laura England Edwards*

Budget and Schedule Planner

Vision: What do you want to achieve?

Start with the end product so you have a clear idea of where you are going. Pictures, sketches and mood boards can help here, and you can refer back to them as you progress and/or use them for motivation.

My Vision

....

....

....

....

....

....

....

....

....

....

Budget

Once you've costed everything you need, start looking for savings wherever possible using the 7 Golden Rules on page 8, including borrowing, reusing, deal-hunting and hiring equipment.

Use the table below to work out your budget.

WHAT YOU NEED	Cost	GOLDEN RULE SAVING OPTION	Savings
	£		£
	£		£
	£		£
	£		£
	£		£
	£		£
	£		£
	£		£
	£		£
TOTAL COST £		TOTAL SAVINGS £	

Total cost – total savings = budget £

Overspend contingency of 10% £

Total £

Schedule

Breaking down your project into tasks and steps can help make larger projects more manageable and less daunting, and can give you a clear path to achieving your goal. If you're short on funds, you can also plan to get to a point where you can enjoy your progress to date while you save towards doing more.

TASKS/STEPS	TARGET COMPLETION DATE
1	
2	
3	
4	
5	
6	
7	
8	
9	
10	

The Bathroom

With the exception of the kitchen, the bathroom is the room of the house that probably receives the most traffic during the day and into the evenings, seven days a week. Chances are, you're in and out of there in a rush in the morning and see the bathroom as a purely functional space, which means it gets forgotten about, slowly growing ever more worn out and mouldy. It doesn't have to be this way – your bathroom can be a wonderfully tranquil space where you can escape the stresses and strains of the day, and unwind with some much-needed peace and quiet. It's well worth taking the time to make this an inviting room, somewhere that fulfils its practical purpose but is also appealing.

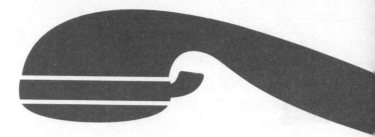

Again, as with the
kitchen, the bathroom
can be one of the most
expensive rooms in the house
to refurbish, but there is so
much you can do to update it
without ripping everything out
and starting from scratch. From
laying new floor or wall tiles, to
putting up mirrors and shelves – even
a budget-friendly refresh of your bath/
shower or toilet can have a huge impact.
In the pages that follow, we'll run through
some essential DIY tips to get you started,
from the basics to essential maintenance
advice that will revive and extend the lifespan
of your bathroom. We'll also cover all the little
jobs you might not have considered that could
transform the whole look of the room.

> **Walls and Floors**

If your bathroom is looking a bit sad and tired, dark and dingy, or just really old fashioned, one way to update its look is by revisiting the walls and floors. You might prefer the timeless look of a wooden floor, classic tiles, or even the contemporary look of some patterned vinyl, but whatever you choose, make sure it's waterproof and properly sealed (see page 48 for how to lay flooring). You can even give your floor an inexpensive lift by stencilling it (see page 214).

Bathroom walls

Tiles are the best option for covering walls in a bathroom, as they're a hardwearing, water-resistant way to protect them from water. With such a huge range of shapes, sizes and styles to choose from, they also give you the ideal opportunity to inject some texture and pattern into your bathroom. Your choice can reflect your personality and create a specific mood. A carefully considered colour can even brighten up a dark room or lift a bland space. For detailed information on tiling, see page 32.

Another popular option for covering bathroom walls is wooden panelling. You can buy this in sheets that you can cut to fit, or as tongue-and-groove pieces that slot together and can be painted to suit your style. Panelling does a great job of protecting the walls around the edge of the bath and the toilet or basin. Remember to use moisture-resistant paint when painting your panelling.

> ### Toni's Top Tip
>
> *If you're fitting wooden panelling or tiles in your bathroom, always make sure to seal along the point at which your floor meets the bottom of your wall fitting. Use a mould-resistant silicone sealant to stop water from getting in.*

If you decide to tile your bathroom, here are a few helpful pointers:

- Decide on which bit of your space you want to tile – if it's a small shower room you might want to tile every wall from floor to ceiling. If it's a larger room, however, you might opt for half tiled, where you tile only around the bath/shower and the basin.

- Think about the mood you want to create in your bathroom, as this will inform your design ideas and choices. Do you want a serene space where you can decompress at the end of the day, or do you have a young and growing family who splash water all over the place and enjoy having white tiles to draw on with bath crayons? (If you have kids who get water everywhere, you might prefer slip-resistant flooring, too.)

> ### Toni's Top Tip
>
> *Don't forget to factor in the cost of adhesive and grouting when you're budgeting for tiling.*

- Measure the bathroom carefully and, in particular, the space you want to tile. Calculate the area in metres squared, so that you can easily cost up your tiles when choosing them.

- Big vs small – in smaller spaces, larger tiles can make a space feel bigger as there are fewer grouting lines, which gives a cleaner, more continuous look. However, smaller tiles can be more versatile – particularly sheets of mosaic tiles – and you can play around with where they go or mix and match them with other patterns.

Toni's Top Tip

If your existing grouting looks a bit grubby but is otherwise intact, you can simply brighten it up with a grouting pen. If the pen's nib splits or stops working while you're using it, cut the pen in half and use a small artist's paint brush to access and use the liquid inside.

> Resealing the Shower or Bath

Over time, the sealant on your shower or bath may start to perish, go mouldy, or even come off in places. Regular cleaning will, of course, help to prolong its lifespan, but ultimately, this kind of wear is inevitable. So, if it's seen better days and nothing you try is making it look any better, it's time to start afresh. You don't need to call someone in to do this, as it's not tricky. In fact, it's a very satisfying job to carry out yourself.

ALLOW TIME FOR . . .

- The sealant to dry and set, which can be up to 48 hours (during which time you can't use your bath or shower)

WHAT YOU NEED

- Anti-mould sealant
- Paint scraper or Stanley knife
- Sponge
- Bathroom cleaner
- Sealant gun
- Disposable gloves (and goggles, to be extra careful)

HOW TO

1   First, buy your sealant. Shop around to find the one that best suits your needs and check the packaging instructions to see where it can be used. Sealant comes in different colours, too, so make sure you buy one that matches your tiles (or offers a contrast, if that's the look you're going for).

2   Now it's time to remove the old sealant. Use a paint scraper or Stanley knife to cut along the top and bottom of the strip, then pull it away. You can scrape away any residue using a scraper, or the blade, but make sure you don't scratch the bath, the shower or the tiles in the process. Easy does it!

Watch Out!

It's really important to allow the sealant to dry properly, and this means you won't be able to use your bath or shower during this time. There's no cutting corners here – if you get the sealant wet before it's fully cured, you'll have to redo it.

3   Once all the sealant and debris have been removed, use a sponge to clean the whole area with warm soapy water and/or a bathroom cleaner. Remove as much grease and grime as you can, otherwise you'll struggle to get a good seal on the new sealant. Allow the whole area to dry completely before moving on to the next step.

4   Applying the new sealant is the trickiest bit, but don't worry, as any mistakes can be fixed! In the same way that you removed the old sealant, you can do the same with the new application if it doesn't go to plan.

5   Fit the tube of sealant into the sealant gun and, with steady pressure, apply a thick line of sealant around the edges of the bath or shower. Try to move at an even speed but don't worry if your bead of sealant is slightly uneven – you can sort that in the next step.

6   It's now time to smooth it out. Wearing your clean disposable gloves, run your finger along the new sealant. Again, use steady pressure and move at an even speed. You need to be fairly quick here as the drier the sealant gets, the less you're able to mould it. If it does start to dry, dab your finger in a bowl of soapy water, then run it over the sealant.

7 Wipe away any excess and let the sealant dry according to the manufacturer's guidelines.

Toni's Top Tip

If you're sealing a bath, fill it up with water before you apply the fresh sealant, and be careful not to get any water on the sealant as it dries. By doing this, the sealant will cure at the position the bath sits in when in use. If the sealant dries when the bath is empty, it can split and come loose once you fill up the tub, as the pressure on its edges increases.

> Changing a Toilet Seat

Over time, toilet seats become worn or damaged, and so it becomes necessary to replace them for practical reasons. However, you can also see it as a fun opportunity to upgrade your bathroom and give it a pop of colour or personality. A huge array of coloured seats are available these days, incorporating all manner of designs, including glitter, stencilling or resin with a shell pattern.

Changing the toilet seat itself is a relatively straightforward task, and it's a useful thing to know how to do, even if you just want to remove it to give it a really good clean. So, here's a quick guide to giving your toilet seat a lift . . .

First things first, you need to find a replacement. Toilets don't just come in one size, so use a tape measure to measure the width, length and distance between fixing holes of your existing toilet seat. For width, measure across the pan at the widest point; for length, measure from between the fixing holes to the front end of your toilet; and finally, measure the distance between the fixing holes.

Once you have your measurements, shop around and see what's available design-wise in that size. You don't just have to go with plain white, and remember, seats come with potentially useful features, such as soft-close lids. Also take a look at the fixtures on your toilet seat – make sure that the new ones match what is there.

Once you've selected your new toilet seat, it's time to fit it. Remove the old seat by loosening the bolts that are securing it – generally, seats are held in place by two bolts under plastic caps at the back of the toilet seat itself. Use a screwdriver to remove these protective caps and you'll see the top of the bolts, underneath which are two nuts. Use your pliers to hold the nuts in place while you unscrew the bolts with your screwdriver or wrench. Some seats will have different fittings, but the same principle applies – you might just need a screwdriver with a different head to remove them, or you might find using a wrench easier.

Now you can fit your new seat. All being well, this step should simply be the last step in the reverse, but double check the instructions from the manufacturer. Tighten the bolts but make sure not to overtighten them, as you may need to adjust the seat once it's in place, and overtightening can damage the fittings.

> Painting Your Toilet

If you're looking for an easy way to breathe new life into your toilet, a lick of paint on it might just do the trick. Whether it's a calm neutral or a shocking pink, this little uplift is an easier job than you might think, but be aware that the drying times of the various layers of paint could mean your toilet is out of action for a couple of days.

ALLOW TIME FOR . . .

- **The paint to dry between coats, plus overnight drying**

WHAT YOU NEED

- **Dust sheets**
- **Painter's tape**
- **Toilet cleaner**
- **Clean cloths**
- **Pliers**
- **Old towels**
- **Safety goggles and face mask**
- **Coarse-grit (40) sandpaper**
- **Acrylic latex primer**
- **Spray paint in your preferred colour**
- **Clear epoxy top coat**

HOW TO

1 Lay your dust sheets on the floor and walls around your toilet, and secure with tape. Ensure the room is well ventilated – open any windows, or the door if there are no windows, and turn on the fan.

2 Clean your toilet using your usual toilet cleaner – as with any other surface, paint won't adhere well to a surface that is dirty or grimy. Flush to rinse the bowl.

3 Remove the toilet seat. Methods vary depending on your seat, but generally you simply unscrew the bolts holding the seat in place. Thoroughly clean any newly exposed areas.

4 Stop the water by shutting off the water valve. You'll find this on the pipe that leads into the cistern (the square bit above the bowl). Now flush the toilet to get rid of any water in the bowl and the cistern. Remove the lid from the cistern to check all the water has drained away. If not, flush again. Dry with an old towel.

5 Pop on your goggles and face mask, and sand every surface of the toilet that you wish to paint. Porcelain is so smooth that paint can struggle to stick to it, so a thorough sanding with coarse-grit (40) sandpaper will change its surface texture and ensure a good finish.

6 Clean the toilet again in order to remove the porcelain dust – wipe it down with a clean damp cloth and dry with an old towel.

7   When the toilet is dry and clean it's time to apply your acrylic latex primer. Make sure all desired areas are covered, then follow the manufacturer's guidelines on the paint tin for drying times.

8   Once the primer is dry, you can add your chosen colour of spray paint. Just like any other type of paint, you'll need to do a few coats to build up the colour, allowing each layer to dry before adding more. Before you start spraying, check that the dust sheets are still firmly in place and covering anything that you don't want to paint!

9   Spray carefully and evenly, then leave to dry according to the drying times on the can.

10   Once the spray paint has dried, apply your clear epoxy top coat to ensure your new paint job is waterproof. For best results, leave this final coat to dry overnight.

11   When it's all dry, reattach your toilet seat (see page 200 for detailed instructions), then, finally, open your water valve and allow the toilet to refill as normal. Give it a flush and then take a look at your cool new focal point.

Toni's Top Tip

It might not be the most exciting prospect in the world but it's not every day you remove your toilet seat, so this is a good opportunity to give it a good clean.

> Fitting Toilet-roll Holders

Having toilet roll to hand on a secure holder is not just convenient, it also means it isn't balanced precariously on the side of the basin or the bath and liable to get soaking wet! Fitting a toilet-roll holder is a really simple job, and well worth half an hour (or less) of your time.

WHAT YOU NEED

- **Toilet-roll holder of your choice**
- **Pipe and cable detector**
- **Spirit level**
- **Pencil**
- **Masking tape**
- **Safety goggles**
- **Safety gloves**
- **Power drill and drill bits suitable for tiles/masonry**
- **Rawl plugs**
- **Screws**
- **Hammer**
- **Screwdriver**

HOW TO

1   Pick a position for your toilet-roll holder, making sure it's within easy reach of the toilet and, to avoid damp toilet roll, not too close to the basin or the bath. If you're not sure, sit on the toilet to see where it would be most convenient to put it!

2 Use a pipe detector to check your chosen area. It's worth taking extra care with this step as you don't want to accidentally drill into a pipe.

3 Hold the wall bracket of your toilet-roll holder in position, use the spirit level to check the top of it is straight, and mark the position of the holes with a pencil.

4 If you're drilling into tiles, cover the area with masking tape first to reduce the risk of slipping while you're drilling, then mark the spot with a pencil. Check the hammer setting is off on your drill for tiles, but if you're drilling through masonry you'll want this setting on. Do a final check of your drill settings, drill bits and rawl plugs – too big and it won't hold, too small and the holder may fall off the wall – then pop on your gloves and goggles and start drilling the holes.

Toni's Top Tip

If you want to know when to stop drilling, use masking tape to mark the depth of the wall plug on the drill bit before you start, then only go that far into the wall.

5 Push your rawl plugs into the holes. If you're working with tiles, use a screw and a hammer to gently tap the plugs below the surface level of the tile – this will prevent the tile from cracking when the plugs expand as you insert the screws. Check the holes are level, then remove the screw and screw the wall bracket firmly in place.

6 Place your new holder onto the brackets and fasten securely by tightening the small grub screw at the bottom.

7 Your toilet-roll holder is now sorted! Pop on a roll and it's good to go.

Toni's Top Tip

It's all in the details. Your bathroom fixtures can help complete the look you're going for, update your bathroom in line with your unique style, or give it a modern lift and feel. When you choose your toilet-roll holder, for example, have a look at what other hardware is in the same design range – there might be toothbrush holders, shelves or soap-dispenser holders, too. Updating all these items will not only give your bathroom a lift but will tie it all together in great style.

> Changing Taps

When you think about how often you use your bathroom taps, it makes sense to install ones that you love. Don't worry, you don't need any plumbing qualifications for this project, just a couple of tools and a bit of time.

WHAT YOU NEED

- Wrench
- Taps of your choice
- Washer (depending on your tap and thread)
- Compression fitting suitable for your taps and your pipes

Watch Out!

Always make sure your mains water is turned off before you change a tap, or things could get very wet and very messy! To do this you need to know where your stopcock is – it's usually under the kitchen sink. If you don't know where it is, now is a really good time to discover this vital information! When you've found it, turn the valve in a clockwise direction. To turn it back on, twist the valve anti-clockwise and let the tap run to allow the water time to run through the system.

HOW TO

1 Begin by turning off your mains water supply (see Watch Out! box above). Then run the taps to drain the system of all the leftover water.

2 Now for the slightly tricky part: get under your basin or your bath and unscrew the nut that is keeping your old

tap locked in place. Once loosened, it should pop right off and you'll be able to lift and remove the old tap.

3   To install the new tap, connect the threaded post (the screw part) to the tap, then feed it through the hole so that your tap is sitting neatly on the sink or bath, with the thread hanging out the bottom.

4   Screw the nut onto the thread, and your new tap should now be fitted tightly. If it feels loose, you might need a washer between the tap and the nut to ensure the tap is secure.

5   Next, connect your plumbing by screwing the flexible connectors to your tap, then attach these to the pipes (likely the copper ones). Use a compression fitting (a safe way to connect copper pipe without the use of heat), and this will keep the pressure between the pipes consistent and safe.

6   Take a step back and check that your tap is firmly attached – if it's left loose there could be leaks.

7   Make sure your tap is set to open, then turn on your water mains supply again. If your tap is closed when the water comes through the pipes, it could damage the new tap. You might hear some air coming through to start with, but be patient, as the water will soon follow.

8   Leave your new tap running for a moment, to check that the water stream is flowing steadily.

9   Your new tap is officially installed – happy washing!

> Hidden Storage Ideas for Bathrooms

Face creams, moisturizers, endless hairbands, spare towels and more. Bathrooms are full of products and paraphernalia, and can quickly become a disorganized space that's overwhelming and hard to clean. Quite aside from that, a long soak in your bath will be a much more enjoyable experience if you're not looking at clusters of shampoo and conditioner bottles.

Regardless of the size of your bathroom, here are some handy storage ideas to keep it clean and clutter free.

1   Hooks are not to be underestimated. They have many uses and installing them is likely the easiest DIY job around. Fixing them to key spots in your bathroom, such as the back of the door or just outside your shower, can keep towels off the floor and within easy reach when you're wet. Don't use them just for towels, though – hooks are the perfect bit of hardware from which to hang dressing gowns, bath brushes or laundry bags.

2   As ever with space-saving ideas, it's all about finding empty spots in a room and using them to your advantage. In your bathroom, it's very likely there's a gap between the top of the door and the ceiling, or even above the bath or the loo, so place a shelf in this location and use it to store items such as toilet rolls, cosmetics or extra towels.

3   A fun project where you can indulge your creative side is repurposing a drinks trolley. This handy item of furniture can be painted with bathroom-friendly paint and

used to house all your bathroom accessories. Add a cute plant pot and a pretty candle, and you've got the perfect combination of storage and style.

4   Shower rails don't have to be just for hanging shower curtains – you can install an extra one over your bath or shower and use it to hang additional items, such as towels. Shower caddies work well as storage options too – hang them along the shower rail or use a drill to fix them into the corner of your shower cubicle, as you did with the toilet-roll holder (see page 204). They can be used for storing shampoo and shower gel within easy reach.

5   The walls in a bathroom can provide storage space too. Drill in and secure some stacking shelves or hanging baskets – the shelves are useful for storing essential items and decorative ones in attractive and practical baskets, while hanging baskets can look lovely when filled with fluffy, rolled towels.

> How to Hang a Mirror

Whatever type of DIYer you are, you'll probably need to hang a mirror at some point. At first glance, it might seem like a nail-in-the-wall job, but, if you want to avoid seven years' bad luck (or, more realistically, a burst pipe), you'll need to follow a few simple steps.

The first thing to find out is the type of wall you're working with, as this will impact the fittings you use to secure the mirror. If you have hollow stud walls, you can use hooks or screws, but if your wall is brick you will likely need masonry nails. If you're hanging something particularly heavy (anything over 15kg), then you should probably use screws and rawl plugs. Often, a mirror will be supplied with fittings, so make sure you use what is recommended. Don't forget that if you're using rawl plugs, you'll also need a drill bit suitable for them.

WHAT YOU NEED

- Stud finder
- Pencil
- Masking tape
- Tape measure
- Spirit level
- Power drill
- Hooks/screws or matching masonry screws, rawl plugs and corresponding drill bit
- Cord or metal wire, for hanging (if needed)

HOW TO

1 Use your stud finder to determine the location of any cables and pipes within the wall, and, if relevant, mark where your studs are.

2 Hold the mirror up to the wall (with the help of another person, if necessary) to decide on its placement, and use masking tape or pencil to mark the area – the top and bottom of the mirror as well as where the fittings need to be attached to the wall to achieve that position.

3 If hanging on a stud wall, drill screws or hooks into the studs themselves.

4 If your mirror has D-rings on it, string a length of cord or metal wire between the two D-rings. If working on a stud wall, your mirror is now ready to hang.

5 If you do not have a stud wall, you'll need to use either masonry nails or screws and rawl plugs. Check the manufacturer's guidelines for guidance on the size of rawl plug and screw required, or seek advice at your local DIY store, making sure to reference the mirror's weight.

6 Using your power drill and drill bit, drill two holes into the brickwork or studs, ensuring you drill deeply enough to fit the rawl plugs, if using.

7 Push the rawl plugs into the holes, then screw in your masonry screws, ensuring enough of them is left exposed from which to hang the mirror.

Watch Out!

Never use Velcro or sticky-backed fixings to hang mirrors! These options can work for very light pictures, but it's not worth the risk here.

If you're hanging a heavy mirror, it's best to secure at least one screw into a stud wall, so it's worth considering if there's any wiggle room with your proposed spot should it fall between two studs.

Watch Out!

Never use water-based paint on tiles in your bathroom – it will deteriorate very quickly!

Leave enough time for each coat of paint and sealant to dry before either applying the next one or walking on the tiles, to avoid ruining your painted stencil design.

Stencilled Bathroom Tiles

Toni's Choice

I've chosen Natalie Jenkins to describe how she totally transformed her bathroom from a cold, boring space into something worthy of a five-star hotel by stencilling intricate mosaic patterns onto the plain painted bathroom tiles. It looks so great, it's almost a shame to put down a bathmat!

WHAT YOU NEED

- Cushion or knee pad
- Cleaning products suitable for your bathroom tiles
- Primer and paint suitable for bathroom floor tiles (see page 217)
- Paint brushes or rollers for painting the floor tiles
- Floor tile stencils to fit your tiles – there are many sizes and designs available online
- Painter's tape
- Small foam roller or stencil brush
- Sealant suitable for the paint used

HOW TO

1 Clean your floor tiles thoroughly and leave enough time for them to dry.

2 Paint the tiles in your chosen colour, and remember to leave enough time between coats for them to dry fully.

3 Starting at one end of the bathroom, position your stencil over a tile and secure it in place with four lengths of painter's tape – one along each edge of the tile.

4 Using your foam roller or stencil brush, paint over the stencil to apply the design to the tile.

5 Gently remove the stencil template and move on to the next tile, repeating the process until you've stencilled all the tiles. Allow to dry overnight for best results.

6 Once you're happy with the stencilling and the paint is fully dry, apply a layer or two of sealant to fully protect your work.

Toni's Top Tip

When working on floor tiles – or doing any work where you have to be on your knees for a long time – why not fold up (or even cut off a section of) a yoga mat? They're great for kneeling on, as well as stretching out on after a long day of DIY!

Member's Method

When we moved into our bungalow eighteen months ago, one of the main jobs we wanted to do was a complete bathroom overhaul. Unfortunately, we also came up against a few unexpected major expenses, so our new bathroom project went out the window. The existing bathroom was so bland and cold-looking that I decided to give it a budget revamp by painting and stencilling the floor tiles. I'd already completed a couple of big stencilling projects at home, and it was something I was keen to do again as it looks so great and costs very little.

I had the stencil customized to the size of my tiles at no extra cost – you can find loads of companies online who will do this. After thoroughly cleaning the floor and leaving it to dry, I secured the stencil to the tile with painter's tape, then painted over it using a minimal amount of paint on a foam roller – this stops it bleeding through the pattern and leaves you with crisp lines. Then I gently lifted the stencil off and did the next tile – I always complete the full-sized tiles first as they're pretty quick and easy to do. I find it's easier to tackle the trickier corner tiles at the end, or you could do them another day, depending on how much patience you have left! Once all the paint was dry, I applied three separate coats of sealant on the tiles. I'd definitely advise using a cushion to kneel on while stencilling the floor – to save your knees!

Members' Top Tips

- Measure the overall area that you want to stencil, so you can decide what size you want the stencil to be and how it will fit in the space. Print out a few sheets and position them over the walls/floor to see how the design might look and how best to position it.

- When you choose your paint colours and paint, remember it needs to be water resistant and hardwearing. Don't use runny paint either, or it might bleed through the pattern.

- Make sure your stencil is taped in place securely and doesn't move while you're painting.

- Use painter's tape to cover any areas that you want to paint a different colour and wait for one colour to dry before painting the next.

- Use a good stencil brush and invest in some decent stencil cleaner to clean and preserve your brush and stencil for future use.

- If you have time, let the paint dry a bit before you remove the stencil. This will help to make sure that you don't accidentally smear or smudge the paint as you lift the stencil away.

- Take your time on the prep work, as it will pay off in the end result and make the stencilling last.

Members' Comments

Wow! Now that's a cracking makeover!!! *Sarah Edwards*

Wow! What a difference. *Marian Milne*

What a fabulous job! Those tiles look totally amazing now.
Well done! *Mary Murdock*

Budget and Schedule Planner

Vision: What do you want to achieve?

Start with the end product so you have a clear idea of where you are going. Pictures, sketches and mood boards can help here, and you can refer back to them as you progress and/or use them for motivation.

My Vision

....

....

....

....

....

....

....

....

....

Budget

Once you've costed everything you need, start looking for savings wherever possible using the 7 Golden Rules on page 8, including borrowing, reusing, deal-hunting and hiring equipment.

Use the table below to work out your budget.

WHAT YOU NEED	Cost	GOLDEN RULE SAVING OPTION	Savings
	£		£
	£		£
	£		£
	£		£
	£		£
	£		£
	£		£
	£		£
	£		£
TOTAL COST £		TOTAL SAVINGS £	

Total cost – total savings = budget £

Overspend contingency of 10% £

Total   £

Schedule

Breaking down your project into tasks and steps can help make larger projects more manageable and less daunting, and can give you a clear path to achieving your goal. If you're short on funds, you can also plan to get to a point where you can enjoy your progress to date while you save towards doing more.

TASKS/STEPS	TARGET COMPLETION DATE
1	
2	
3	
4	
5	
6	
7	
8	
9	
10	

Bedrooms

Your bedroom – a safe haven away from work, stress and worry; a place where you can switch off, relax and recharge your batteries. In theory, anyway. For many of us, our bedroom has had to become a multi-purpose space in recent years, doubling up as a temporary office, gym or even storage area, and, as a result, it can be easy to lose that sense of serenity that comes with having our own private space. Despite spending more hours in our bedroom than in any other room of the house, there are probably very few of us who don't look at their own bedroom, the kid's room or a spare, and think it could do with some improvement.

So, in this section, we want to present to you some of the many possibilities when it comes to transforming a bedroom without breaking the bank. Love the idea of built-in wardrobes but don't want to spend a fortune? Have a go at building some yourself. Want to bring some boutique-hotel vibes to your evenings? We'll show you how to add a touch of glamour with a chic homemade headboard. There are also some creative ideas for including some hidden storage. We haven't forgotten children, either, so you'll find some ideas for bedroom spaces that will take your kids from their nursery years to their teenage ones, without the need for huge and expensive revamps.

> Built-in Wardrobes

For many, fitted wardrobe spaces are the ideal bedroom-storage set-up, but getting them professionally built and installed can make a dent in your wallet. You might think that building some yourself is outside the realms of possibility, but don't rule it out. Of course, it can be a big job, requiring a number of tools and materials, and so it might be a reach for absolute beginners without some assistance. However, no matter your DIY skill level, you can learn a lot from watching online tutorials or from following advice from more experienced individuals who've completed similar projects.

So, if you want to give it a go and have a suitable space you've always wanted to convert, the handy guide that follows will give you some pointers to steer you in the right direction. Because of the massive variations in individual requirements, an exact step-by-step guide is

near impossible to make practical, so here are some handy
dos and don'ts to help you plan ahead. The possibilities
are endless in terms of the design, so do some research for
inspiration, or look up how others have converted their own
similar spaces.

> Dos and Don'ts

DO Measure, measure, measure
- Decide where in your room you'll be building the
  wardrobes – perhaps along a side wall, or maybe you
  have a natural alcove to the side of a chimney breast.
  You'll want to take as many measurements as possible
  for the space, including its height, width and depth,
  depending on how deep you want your wardrobes to
  be. If you're working in an attic space with a sloping
  ceiling, you'll need to take even more measurements to
  gauge the pitch of the ceiling.

DON'T Overlook the previous step
- One of the most common problems you'll encounter is
  not having taken precise measurements, which means
  you'll have to bodge the job midway to rectify your
  mistake.

DO Make a plan
- You might want to work with some design software or
  enlist help from someone who can assist you with this
  part of the process. By creating an accurate plan of
  your space, it will be much easier to envisage how you
  want to build your wardrobe. Your best bet is to keep
  things simple. You'll need to fit a base frame to the floor,

which you can build on, with a simple interior frame, and within that any cupboard spaces or shelves. Finally, you'll need to decide whether you want double or single doors. Think about any trimmings you might want at the top, bottom and sides of the doors, too – these can all be created effectively with MDF.

DON'T Attempt this project without the right tools

- To make cuts of MDF (or other affordable materials) that need to be fitted together in a precise manner, you're going to have to achieve a high level of accuracy. You need to be exact, even if you're working with a precision tool such as a circular or table saw, so consider getting your local DIY store to cut the boards to size for you.

DO Look at upcycling existing furniture

- A lot of people have had great success using existing items of furniture, such as dressers and drawers, to use as a frame to build around. It can be a really good way to avoid having to build an entire set of wardrobes from scratch, and allows you to create a plan based on existing furniture.

DON'T Make your compartments too big

- If your individual sections exceed a metre in width, consider breaking them down into smaller cabinets. Keep the width of each door less than 50cm, as this will make them easier to work with. It's also worth remembering that if your doors are too big, you may struggle to open them fully while still having enough space in the rest of the room. Another issue to consider is the strength of the shelving boards. If any of your horizontal pieces are over 50cm wide, choose boards that are thicker than 1.5cm because, over time and with loads on them, anything thinner than that can start to sag.

DO Think about your doors

- Many people go for open wardrobes, which look great, but if you're going traditional and putting on doors, fitting them well might prove the most difficult part of the project. Building a frame is relatively straight forward but doors, particularly if you're working with a sloping ceiling in an attic space, can be much trickier. Work out how the doors will hang by taking careful and accurate measurements, and ensure you factor in enough space for them to open and close properly – and that includes sufficient clearance for them to skim over any carpet on the floor.

- It's worth remembering that each door shouldn't be exactly half the width of the total span of the cabinet, as the fit would be too tight and probably wouldn't even close. Standard recommended gaps for cupboard doors are 2mm on each side and 2.5mm on the top and the bottom. Also, don't forget to choose hinges that are strong enough to hold the weight of each door. Hanging doors can be difficult, so make sure to enlist someone's help – even if it's just to support the weight of the door – and take your time to get it right. Drilling pilot holes for any screws you use is always useful.

DON'T Forget to finish your MDF

- You don't want any rough edges, so if you're using MDF you'll need to sand, seal and paint it thoroughly. You might end up needing several coats, but the end result will be a much better finish.

DO Get help

- All of the materials together will be incredibly heavy, so help to carry them to the bedroom will be a real bonus, as will a second pair of eyes and support – moral or otherwise! Two heads are better than one.

DON'T Try this on a whim

- Be under no illusion – building a wardrobe is a big job and can take a long time if you're a total novice. That isn't to say it's impossible, but a rainy Sunday afternoon won't quite cut it.

> **Building a Bed**

While you can end up spending a fortune on buying a new bed, too many people try to save money and sacrifice comfort by continuing to use a tired old frame. Surely anything is better than that? Bed frames can be picked up for very little nowadays, but this idea could see you make your own for nothing!

So, why not have a go at building your own pallet bed? This simple guide gives you the rough steps to making your own, from recycled pallets, with some key tips and things to consider. It's important to take all the necessary steps to make your bed safe and secure, and, most of all, level, so you don't cause problems for yourself. The end result is definitely nothing fancy, but it's much easier than you might think.

You can acquire pallets from lots of different places – sure, you can buy them, but you can often pick them up for free through local listings on Facebook Marketplace or Gumtree. It's also worth enquiring at local stores to see if they have any they're getting rid of. Don't settle for any old pallets, though – you need to make sure they're in good condition, they aren't broken or have any nails or screws sticking out of them, and that they're all the same size. You'll need four pallets for a double bed, but if you're making any other size, just make sure that when they're put together, the pallets are larger than your mattress.

ALLOW TIME FOR . . .

- **The paint to dry between coats, and overnight drying**

WHAT YOU NEED

- **4 pallets (for a double bed)**
- **Medium-grit (80) and fine-grit (120) sandpaper**
- **Primer**
- **Large paint brush**
- **Heavy-duty wood paint in your preferred colour**
- **Connector plates (about 24)**
- **Power drill**
- **Screws**

HOW TO

1   Decide how you want your bed to look. If you want a painted finish, it's a good idea to prep and paint your pallets before you assemble them, as it will be much easier and less messy than doing it in situ.

2 Pallets are generally very roughly finished, so prep them by sanding them down, first with medium-grit then fine-grit sandpaper, and removing any nails, screws or other sharp bits that might be sticking out of them. Run the nozzle attachment on the vacuum over the surfaces to get rid of any residual dust, ready for them to be primed.

Toni's Top Tip

If your bed is going to sit on top of carpet, you won't need to worry too much about preparing its base. However, if your flooring is wood or laminate, you might want to add large felt pads, or even lockable castors to the underside of the base, to protect your floor.

3 If you're painting the pallets, apply a layer of primer with a paint brush and allow this to fully dry, before painting another coat, this time using a heavy-duty wood paint in the colour of your choice. Leave to dry, then decide whether you need one final coat to build up the colour. (If your pallets are much bigger than the mattress, this will create a striking platform look in your room, so painting them the same colour as the woodwork in the bedroom, such as skirting boards, door and door frames, would unify the colour scheme.) If you're not painting your pallets, you can skip this step.

4 Lay the four pallets on the floor of your bedroom, in position, face down. Attach them to one another

by positioning the connector plates along the four connecting sides – around five or six per pallet length, depending on the size of your pallets – and pre-drill holes ready for the screws. Ideally, you should countersink the screws here so that the screwheads don't stick out of the wood, but it's not absolutely necessary to do so. To strengthen your structure, fix the plates in place using long screws, and to make the bed base even more rigid you can also fix plates across the centre pallets as well.

Toni's Top Tip

You could even fashion a makeshift headboard out of extra pallets. Get hold of two more identical ones, prep them, and attach them to one end of your structure. If necessary, cut them down to size, but take care when doing so, and sand them down fully to finish them.

> Headboards

As modern trends have seen people opting for more minimal bed-frame options and a cleaner look, headboards, for many, have become a thing of the past. However, they can be a colourful way to add texture and style to a bedroom, and even a little bit of luxury. Best of all, you don't have to spend a fortune on something that isn't quite right for you – there are a number of budget DIY options out there that can be created in an afternoon and tailored perfectly to your style. Have a good look online for inspiration, but here are a few really popular ideas . . .

Painted headboard

If you don't have the funds or the space to fit a new headboard, why not paint one instead? Simply paint a rectangle, or any other shape you fancy, on the wall behind your bed. Use a pencil and a long ruler to mark the outline (or a template if your shape doesn't have regular edges). Use painter's tape to ensure the line around the edge is nice and straight, then paint inside the block. If your walls are a light shade, perhaps go for a bold, contrasting colour. Dark wall? Think light and bright, to draw the eye. Obviously, this isn't a good idea if you like to move your bed round the room occasionally!

Plywood headboard

Get the Scandi look! Measure the size you want and then buy a suitable piece of wood – ideally from somewhere that offers a cutting service.

Macramé headboard

Bring new textiles into your room by creating a headboard using a sheet of macramé knotting the width of the bed. Simply attach a wooden batten to the wall above the bed, attach the macramé piece, and allow it to hang down behind the bed.

Noticeboard headboard

Buy yourself some pegboard or corkboard sheets that can be attached to the wall behind your bed. You can then use peg baskets or pins to attach mementos to them. If you like, they can double up as a useful alternative to a bedside table, with handy places for your books, alarm clocks or water bottles.

Salvaged, upcycled headboard

In truth, anything can be a headboard, whether that's a couple of old pallets or some pieces of wood that originally had a different purpose. If you like it, go for it! Just make sure to sand and treat your wood so it's safe to use. Nobody wants a splinter in their head.

Fabric or tapestry headboard

Bring some boho style into your bedroom with a piece of fabric or tapestry. You don't need to be a sewing expert to make your own fabric-covered headboard, or update an old one, as you can use strong glue or a staple gun to secure the material in place. If you're making your own from scratch, make sure you attach some cushioning to a wooden board first, using adhesive or similar, then find a piece of fabric you like the look of that is big enough to cover the front, top and sides of the board. Pull it tight and use staples to fix it to the back of the board. Or hang it from a curtain pole fixed above the bed for a more regal feel.

> <u>Underbed Storage</u>

More storage is always a bonus in any room of the house, but particularly so in bedrooms. There are often loads of unused spaces in a bedroom that can be transformed into handy storage solutions – you just need to think creatively. If your bed is off the floor and you don't have an ottoman or divan base with drawers, you'll likely have a handy space underneath it or an assortment of unwanted items crammed under there as there's nowhere else for them to go. You can buy boxes that slide into the space, or you can pack the assorted bits and pieces into vacuum storage bags, but purpose-made storage is always going to be better aesthetically and in terms of organization. So, what are your options?

Storage baskets

Whether wicker, metal or fabric, baskets can be a great option and have a rustic, homely feel. Simply measure your available space – height, width and depth – and shop around to find baskets that suit your needs. Pay particular attention to their depth, and whether your bed has a lip underneath it that might make it difficult to slide the baskets underneath.

Rolling drawers

A number of affordable ready-made boxes and drawers on wheels, which you can slide under your bed, are now available for purchase. The downside is that they aren't custom-made for your space, so you may have to compromise on some level in order for them to fit, and they might not end up looking as slick as you'd like.

Plastic bags and boxes

While this isn't the most aesthetically pleasing solution, it's definitely a budget-friendly option, as there's a huge range of really cheap bags and boxes on the market that you can use to tidy away your things and put under your bed. These are less user-friendly as they're not on wheels or as accessible, but given what an inexpensive option they are, your budget will likely stretch a long way.

> Building Underbed Storage

If you fancy a project that will result in bespoke underbed storage, have a go at building some of your own drawers. The beauty of this idea is that they'll fit your exact space and will be in a style that you love.

WHAT YOU NEED

- ■ **Tape measure**
- ■ **Wood or other materials (12mm MDF is a cheap and easy-to-use option)**
- ■ **Saw – circular, mitre or handsaw (or you can always choose to have the pieces cut for you at your local DIY store)**
- ■ **Drill and drill bits**
- ■ **Strong wood glue**
- ■ **Screws**
- ■ **Fine-grit (120) sandpaper**

HOW TO

1 Measure the height from your floor to the bottom of the base of your bed (taking into account whether the sides of the bed are lower around the edges and reduce this space, as this will impact whether you can slide out the drawers). Consider whether you'll want to add castors for ease of sliding the drawer out from under the bed, and if so, take the height of the castors into consideration when calculating the height of your drawer(s). Then measure the length of the space between the headboard and footboard legs.

2 Decide how many drawers you want, then use your measurements from step one to calculate how wide your drawers will be, allowing for appropriate clearance around each one. (You'll need at least 10mm of space around them.) Finally, measure how deep you want your drawers to be. You might want to be able to pull one out on each side, or decide that you'd like to pull a larger single drawer from just one side.

3 Measure and mark your pieces of MDF. For each drawer, you will need a base (the full depth and width of the drawer), left and right sides (the full depth of the drawer), and a front and back panel (which need to be the width of the base minus the thickness of the two side panels – it's much better to have the front and back panels sit inside the side pieces when you join them together as, when you're pulling the drawer out, this will result in less stress on the joint over time.

4 Once you have your measurements, you can buy the wood and cut it to size, if you have the appropriate tools. This may require the use of a circular or table saw alongside a mitre or handsaw, but if you don't have access to these tools, your local DIY shop might offer a cutting service, if you supply a detailed cutting list.

5 It's time to start fitting the pieces together. First, attach a front panel and one of the side pieces onto the base of the drawer in a butt joint. Make sure the pieces are flush, then drill two thin pilot holes through the side piece and into the edge of the front panel. Apply wood glue along the joins and secure the panels together with two screws through the corner joint. Do the same for the other corners, and you have the frame for the drawer.

6 Flip your frame over and attach the base panel. Apply a bead of wood glue all along the frame edge then place your base on top so it sits flush with the edges. Drill pilot holes into the frame and secure with screws. Two on each side will be adequate.

7 You've got your drawer, now tidy up the woodwork! Even with the best cutting service and the steadiest of hands, you might be left with some untidy edges or joins, so go over the drawer with sandpaper to ensure a smooth finish.

Finishing touches

• Decide how you want to open your drawer(s). A wide range of handles can be attached to the front panel using screws, or you could use a jigsaw to create a cut-out handle at the top of the front panel. If you do the latter, make sure to sand down the edge afterwards to prevent splinters!

- Finish the wood with a couple of coats of paint or an appropriate wood finish. Not only will it personalize the drawers in the style you want, it will also ensure their longevity.

- Get your hands on a pack of castors and fit them to the underside of the drawers. This will make pulling them out a much smoother process, particularly if you have wooden floors. They cost very little, and there are even wheels available specifically for underbed boxes. You'll need four wheels per drawer, and you should attach them flush to the underside of the base, one in each corner, set slightly in from the sides.

> Mini Dressing Room

A separate dressing room is the absolute dream for most women – and men, for that matter – but it remains out of reach for those of us who are already using almost every last inch of our homes. If you're lucky, you could use a tiny box room near the master bedroom as the perfect dedicated dressing room, or a corner of your bedroom or an alcove. Here are a few other easy ideas to give you your own separate dressing space without needing to renovate the house.

Use a hanging curtain or a screen to create a divide

Pair a chest of drawers or a wardrobe with a console table and a mirror, and close the arrangement off from the rest of the room by hanging a length of fabric from a ceiling pole or by using a freestanding screen divide. It's a really simple way to create some privacy and can be done for very little.

Use furniture to divide the room

If your room is fairly spacious, you could move your freestanding wardrobes or other floor-to-ceiling storage units to the centre of the space, creating a natural partition between your bed and sleeping zone on one side, and your dressing-room area on the other.

Transform your built-in cupboard or large wardrobe

If you're fortunate enough to have a large or built-in wardrobe, try adding a mirror and some hanging storage to the inside of one of the doors. Pick up a second-hand stool that you can place in front of the mirror when you open the door, and you've got yourself a makeshift dresser.

Convert an alcove

Sloped ceilings in rooms at the top of a house can be a frustrating feature to deal with when you can't use all of the available floor space, but you could use a natural alcove to create a mini dressing room. Wall-mount rails to save on space, and add a low dressing table and stool towards the end of the area to create a separate dressing zone.

Create a dressing-room wall

If you have the space, use the area in between two wardrobes or cupboards as a mini dressing space that would otherwise become a dumping area. Use brackets to wall-mount a shelf or work surface in between, and hang a mirror. Consider installing a floor-to-ceiling shoe rack on the side of one of the wardrobes and add some battery-powered lighting to build a budget shoe cabinet.

> Bedroom Lighting

Getting the lighting right in a room can make or break the mood, and this is particularly true for a bedroom. You'll want it to be a peaceful space at night, where you can eventually drift off to sleep. For most people, the bedroom needs gentle illumination rather than bright glaring lights, although you might want stronger lighting options in certain corners of your room, such as at a dressing table. Layering your lights – think overhead lights, lamps, spotlights – will help you to bring the right energy to the room when you need it.

Planning your lighting is just as important as planning all the other design features of your bedroom. Here are a few ideas to help you bring it all together.

- If you're short on space and can't accommodate bedside tables, go for a wall-hung lamp on either side of your bed instead, or even pendant lamps that hang from the ceiling. You can even fit spotlights into a homemade

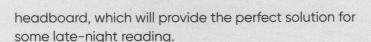

headboard, which will provide the perfect solution for some late-night reading.

- In larger rooms, freestanding floor lamps can be a cosy option, or table lamps set on bedside tables. They can be simple and functional, or you can go all out with statement lamps that become the focal items in the room.

- LED spotlights set into a frame around a mirror can be the perfect way to create a brightly lit corner where you can apply your make-up, and can give a real Hollywood feel to the room!

- An overhead light is always useful, and you can go as bold or as functional as you like when it comes to choosing a shade for it. If you want to vary the light levels in your room at night and then again during the day (particularly if the room is multi-functional), a dimmer switch is a really good solution, but don't try changing switches yourself – this is a job for a qualified electrician.

Toni's Top Tip

If you're renting and can't change the light fittings in your room, you can still adjust the light level by changing the bulbs – a warmer, yellow light will promote relaxation, while a white one will inhibit sleep. LED bulbs are the most energy efficient and emit light that is closest to natural light.

Lighting ideas for kids' rooms

- Fairy lights for the win! No matter what age your kids are, fairy lights give a comforting glow, particularly for children who don't like sleeping in the dark – although only fairy lights with LED bulbs can be left on overnight as they don't emit heat and therefore don't pose a fire hazard. A huge range is available, with and without shades, as well as different-coloured bulbs, so you can change them up to suit your child's changing/growing moods!

- If your older child has a little desk space, a task light is really useful when it comes to doing homework, or to help focus when building Lego creations or model aeroplanes!

- You can also buy strip LED lighting with a sticky back that you can apply directly to the wall and it won't leave a mark (so it's a perfect temporary option for party lighting too!). You can buy these strips online, and some even come with a remote control to change the colours and display settings. They're pretty inexpensive and so easy to install – you just need a plug.

Toni's Top Tip

Wrap short strings of LED fairy lights around wire hangers twisted into shapes such as stars, moons and balloons. Hang them on the wall for a cheap and fun feature.

Watch Out!

·······································

Bulbs can get hot, so don't use hanging pendants in children's rooms within their reach, to avoid accidents.

Regularly check fairy lights for wear and tear: worn plugs, missing light globes and frayed cords can cause electrical faults that can start house fires.

> Nurseries and Kids' Bedrooms

They're your little angels . . . but what is less than angelic is the amount of money they seem to cost you! Of course, we all love our children, but the endless quantities of food, clothes, toys, school supplies, more food, sports gear and, yes, even more food, make a significant dent in the bank balance. The thought of spending additional sums on their bedroom can be difficult to swallow at times, especially with the knowledge that in a year or so they'll have inevitably outgrown their room's current theme or style.

When all is said and done, we know how important it is to provide a safe space for our children – somewhere they can feel secure and happy, have fun, learn and grow. This section is all about how to achieve just that, but on a budget. Making savvy choices when it comes to shopping and decorating means that, with some adaptations, their bedrooms will last them much longer.

> Nurseries

For most of us, welcoming our first child is one of the most important moments we will ever experience – it's really exciting but also nerve-racking. We want everything to be perfect before they arrive and turn our world upside down, which is why getting ahead of the game and sorting out their nursery is no doubt a top priority as their due date nears.

If you're lucky enough to have a separate room for your new arrival, and they won't be sharing with you after those first few months, here are some considerations for creating a cosy space for them.

Practicality

- The decision about where your baby will sleep might already have been made for you, depending on the layout of your home, but if they're going into a separate room, ideally make it one that isn't far from your own bedroom and is nice and quiet.

- If the room gets a lot of light, consider hanging some blackout blinds or curtains.

- Temperature is important – if the room gets very cold, ensure you have adequate heating. On the flipside, if it's a bit of a suntrap, make sure it can be kept suitably cool and well ventilated in the warmer months.

- Keep in mind how long the room will be used as a nursery and how you will adapt it as your child grows up. If you aren't blessed with lots of space, you'll have to balance functionality with longevity.

Safety

- Remove anything from the room that could fall from a height, be grabbed by the child, is dangerous or simply unsuitable for a baby to be around.

- The baby's cot must conform to British Safety Standards BS EN 716:2008 or equivalent safety standards applicable in whichever country you are reading this book, a detail that should be stated in the manufacturer's information. Additionally, the distance between the top of the mattress and the top of the cot sides should be at least 50cm, the cot bars should be vertical, and the distance between them should be no more than 6.5cm.

- Never put the cot by a radiator, heater, strong lamp or a sunny window, and make sure that there are no curtain cords, ribbons, blinds and so on that your baby could get caught up in. If your blinds have cords, cut them so they are not looped.

Watch Out!

While a second-hand cot is fine for your baby on the basis that it meets your country's safety standards, always buy a new mattress, even if the one it comes with looks clean. This is the advice of the Foundation for the Study of Infant Deaths, which has found that a used mattress increases the chances of Sudden Infant Death Syndrome (SIDS), or cot death.

> Decorating Ideas

Decorating the nursery will play to your nesting instincts and can be an opportunity to use your imagination, seeing everything through the eyes of your soon-to-be newborn baby. But don't worry if you're too exhausted by the pregnancy to start decorating – your baby won't judge you! Here are some ideas to help you plan for your all-important arrival.

- **Keep it neutral.** Your colour scheme doesn't have to be pink or blue. Opt for tranquil tones instead – an early years nursery is not the place for bold colours. It is a place for washable paint, though . . .

- **Introduce colour in fun ways.** You could paint geometric shapes on the walls, go for block colouring, or consider wall stickers, which can be picked up really cheaply and will add some playfulness to the room. Think animals or quirky shapes to pique your child's interest.

- **Consider the rest of your home decor.** It's best to follow the themes you've chosen elsewhere. If you've gone for a clean and contemporary look, then carry that style into your baby's room.

- **Adaptability is key.** This room will probably need to change over time as your child gets older. It's therefore a good idea not to double down on baby-specific decor. Instead, opt for a neutral scheme that will allow you to change it as they grow (see page 250).

Toni's Top Tip

If your children share a room but are desperate for their own space, you can easily make a room divider using shelving units, or buy freestanding or ceiling-hung partitions from homeware stores. You can even hang a curtain across the ceiling which can double up as a room divider and a makeshift theatre to encourage their amateur dramatics!

> Themed Rooms

Deciding on how best to decorate your child's bedroom can be a decision-making minefield. You want to create a space they love and can have fun in, but you don't want to find yourself being pestered to change it soon after because your little one's decided they don't like it any more.

You might decide the key is to keep the colour scheme neutral wherever you can, so that you can easily adapt, transform and redesign the room as your child gets bigger, but where's the fun in that? Picking a strong theme can be a really creative way to make their room somewhere special to rest and play. It doesn't always have to be expensive or wasteful when it comes to materials, and by using more temporary decor you can tone the theme up and down as your child gets older, depending on what they want.

Popular theme ideas

Kids love themed rooms, and they're usually quick to tell you what they love most, making it easier for you to create a theme that matches their passion. Here are just a few ideas that have worked well in my experience and that of the DIY OAB family.

- **Intergalactic mission.** This is a great theme for any child, and doesn't mean you have to paint the walls dark (although, of course, you could!). Stick glow-in-the-dark stars to the ceiling and hang model planets from self-adhesive hooks using lengths of string. You can also find really affordable star projectors or nightlights to create the ultimate night sky on their ceiling.

- **Explorer's hut.** Pair camping themed lamps with compass and map stencils on the walls. You can even buy old Ordnance Survey maps at car boot sales or from junk shops and glue them to the walls. Build a simple canopy above the bed with fabric hung from the ceiling or draped over wooden rods fixed to the wall. Your child will feel as if they're going to sleep in a tent every night! The bed-canopy idea is also a really good one that can be adapted as they get older, when you perhaps want to tone down the rest of the explorer theme.

- **Football crazy.** If they're already mad for the game, it's likely that passion won't be going away any time soon. Frame prints or posters of their favourite players and hang their team shirts on the walls. Finish off the scheme with an affordable football- or pitch-shaped rug for the floor.

- **Multi-colour madness.** Keep the walls neutral but turn the room into a Technicolor den, with bold primary-colour shelves and vibrant bedding. You could even replace drawer handles and knobs on the furniture with multi-coloured ones. Add some colourful string lights to keep it bright in the evenings.

- **Cloud castle.** This is a lovely idea for all children. Keep your walls and furniture white to give the illusion of the room being in the clouds. Hang a voile canopy from the ceiling above the bed and track down the fluffiest white rug you can find. Suspend fairy lights from the ceiling, and trail them round the edges of the room. If you really want to double down, you can purchase fake cloud stickers for very little, to dot around the walls.

- **Jungle retreat.** Opt for a lot of wood or wood-veneer furniture to echo the trunks of the trees in the rainforest. Upcycled second-hand pieces work perfectly here, to keep things lush and jungly. Cuddly animal toys and stickers of trees and jungle creatures, paired with fake foliage dotted across the walls out of reach, will create the feeling of a treetop-style escape.

- **Mountain adventure.** This is a great option if you want to bring in a neutral theme. Paint the walls pale blue, then use painter's tape to create a mountain skyline of snowy peaks – add tall, overlapping triangles and zig-zags below the summits. Paint the slopes of the mountains in one or multiple tones of dark grey and use white for the peaks. If the room isn't too big, you might even get away with using sample paint pots!

- **Walls, walls, walls.** Rather than being a specific theme, this is a reminder that there's so much you can do with your child's walls. Chalkboard paint is a really fun option (see page 182) but you can also buy magnetic paint, which means you can then use magnetic sheets on the walls for a fun, evolving feature, as well as using them to stick Lego sheets or cork boards to the wall. These additions can cost very little – the price of the sheets and some adhesive – but can take your child's play, and their imaginations, to another level!

Toni's Top Tip

To wash and disinfect Lego, or any other small toys, put them in a laundry bag or pillowcase, secure the opening and run them through a cleaning cycle in the dishwasher (or washing machine). Remember to remove them before the drying cycle kicks in, and leave them to air dry on a towel.

Designing a room that can grow with your children

Kids grow – as do their tastes and needs – so their bedrooms will probably be the ones that require redecorating most often. Here are a few tips to help you ensure their room grows with them (and save you some expense).

- Go for neutral colours – this advice doesn't just apply to the walls, it goes for the furniture and any chairs, too. Sticking to one colour that can serve as the background for different duvet sets and details will save you a lot of work, not to mention a small fortune in paint costs.

- Don't spend too much on wall decorations – keep these cheap and cheerful, as your kid's favourite TV character will likely change as fast as you change the channel. Peelable stickers are a great idea – you can swap them out easily without having to repaint the wall.

- Buy a bed that will grow with your child. Various toddler beds are available that convert simply into single beds when the time comes and will save you from having to buy a new bed every few years.

- Inject some personality and sense of change into the room with new cushion covers, bedding and accessories. The bed is often the big focal point of a bedroom and can be updated inexpensively.

- Tiny wardrobes are cute, but they don't last long! In just a few short years, your child will need much more space for more clothes, school uniform, PE kit, coats . . . Think ahead and purchase furniture that will stay with them as they grow. You can always upcycle pieces, which is a lot cheaper than buying everything new.

- Consider using a desk to serve first as a changing table, then as a games area for your young child. It can finally be used as a writing surface when they start getting homework.

Toni's Top Tip

Buy a large noticeboard and hang it from the wall. Encourage your kids to pin all their posters and nick-nacks on it, to spare your walls from being covered in blue putty tack or tape marks. This is an especially helpful idea if you're in rented accommodation!

> Murals

If you're not naturally the arty type, the idea of designing a mural might make you feel more than a bit wobbly. However, there are loads of different ways to create a mural in your home, including plenty of options that require absolutely no design input from you. They can be a lovely personal touch in a kids' room, and if your child wants a particular theme, it can be an inexpensive way to update a room as they grow older and want their room to grow with them. Don't let the kids have all the fun, though – the ideas below can be adapted for grown-ups' rooms, too!

Whether you create your mural using a pre-designed template, or one that is specially made from stickers or paints, the very first step is the same . . . prepare your wall! Use soapy water and a clean cloth to thoroughly clean the area. Then, once the space is dry, sand away any lumps and bumps, as these will look particularly obvious underneath a mural. If you find any holes, chips or dips in the plaster, you might need to use wall filler to achieve an even finish. This can be applied in layers using a putty knife, then sanded back to a level surface. Give the wall another wipe with a clean damp cloth and leave to dry. Now your wall is clean, smooth and dry, add a coat of primer to seal it, then allow to dry completely before you apply your mural.

There are a couple of options from this point: the peel-and-stick murals you can buy ready-made, or you can get crafty and paint your own unique and personal bit of art.

If you're applying a peel-and-stick mural:

1 Choose your mural design first – for a kids' room it could be a woodland scene, a geometric pattern, or even a favourite family picture. Think about what your child might like and

what might grow with them – for a little while, at least! Do some online research, perhaps, to find a design you love.

2 Measure your wall dimensions, and then measure again. You want to make sure you order the right size before you part with your cash for your peel-and-stick masterpiece!

3 The mural will likely arrive as a series of panel stickers. Unfurl and measure them before marking on the wall where you will hang the first panel (the easiest option is to mark a panel length along from the edge of the wall).

4 For the actual hanging, you'll probably need an extra pair of hands. Remove a small section of the backing paper and position the panel at the very top of the wall, or wherever you've made your marks, before smoothing it down and into place.

5 Repeat with all other panels until you've finished. Use an old loyalty card to smooth out any bubbles that might have snuck in during application.

Toni's Top Tip

You can also use sticker sets to achieve a mural effect! These are readily available online, made up of several smaller individual stickers, and allow you to create your own scene. Make sure to spend some time planning where you're going to put each one before you fix them to the wall. Otherwise, they're super quick and easy!

> **Painted Murals**

If you have artistic flair, you could try painting your own mural for a truly one-of-a-kind result.

ALLOW TIME FOR . . .

- **The paint to dry**

WHAT YOU NEED

- **String or pencil (to transfer the design)**
- **Brushes (a variety of sizes and tips)**
- **Stepladder**
- **Latex or water-based paints**
- **Bucket of water**
- **Clean cloths**

HOW TO

1   The first step is to decide on your design – no matter how big or small, you need a clear idea of what you're doing before you get going. Sketch it on a piece of paper or design it online – whatever suits you best.

2   You'll then need to scale your design to fit your wall. To do this, draw a grid over your design lightly, ensuring the boxes are all the same size. Then, using either string or pencil markings, replicate the grid on your wall, ensuring it has the same number of boxes. That way, based on the

grid method, you'll know exactly how large each element should be.

3 Once you're ready to begin painting, outline the larger elements of your design on the wall. You'll discover at this point whether your grid system has worked and whether everything is in perspective, as it should be. Don't worry if you make a mistake – just wash off your outline and start again.

4 If you're happy with how your outlines look, fill in the major shapes of your mural and allow the paint to dry. Remember to clean your brushes every time you start using a new colour.

5 Finally, add the smaller elements and details. Take your time when it comes to these, and keep stepping back from the wall to ensure your overall design is coming together as you imagined.

Toni's Top Tips

Keep your brushes clean! It's important to do this no matter what you're painting, but when creating a mural, you might need to use the same brush with different colours, so keep a bucket of water and some clean cloths handy.

If you choose to paint your mural in a high-maintenance area, such as the kitchen or bathroom, use enamel paints for a more durable end result.

Timber Headboard

Toni's Choice

There were so many projects to choose from for this section, but I've chosen the headboard made by James Weir, based on his girlfriend's design, as a headboard is something that can be adapted to suit any style of bedroom. I love the fact that James tried doing it one way first, but he and his girlfriend weren't happy with the result, so he adapted the design. We've all been there, done that!

WHAT YOU NEED

- **Tape measure**
- **Lengths of timber boards, cut to size to suit the width of your bed**
- **Wooden battens measured to suit the height of the headboard**
- **Jigsaw (unless you have the timber and battens cut to size at a DIY store)**
- **Medium-grit (80) and fine-grit (120) sandpaper**
- **Wood stain or paint, depending on the finish you would like**
- **Paint brush**
- **Hammer and nails**
- **Power drill, screws and rawl plugs for brick walls**
- **Coat hooks – enough to suit your design**
- **Needle and thread**
- **Ribbon, decorative rope or lengths of fabric, to sew onto your cushions as loops**
- **Fairy lights**

HOW TO

1 Measure the width of your bed and cut the timber boards to the size of headboard you would like. Cut the battens to your desired headboard height.

2 Sand the timber boards to a smooth finish, starting with medium-grit sandpaper then moving to fine grit. Vacuum the dust away and wipe the boards with a clean damp cloth. Allow the wood to dry, then paint the boards using wood stain or paint, depending on the look you're trying to achieve. Give the boards enough time to dry before you fix them to the wall.

3   Using a hammer and nails for plasterboard or wooden walls, or a power drill, screws and rawl plugs for brick walls, attach the battens to the wall behind your bed – make sure you've got the bed in the position you want it, as fixing the headboard to the wall makes this a fairly permanent commitment! Affix three battens in a vertical position: two at the outside edges of the headboard and one in the centre.

4   Using a hammer and nails, affix the timber boards to the battens in a horizontal arrangement.

5   Screw the coat hooks into the timbers in a position that will enable you to hang your cushions from them.

6   Create loops on your cushions by sewing either ribbon, decorative rope or lengths of fabric to them, then hang them from the coat hooks.

7   Drape your fairy lights around the top edges of the boards and the coat hooks – ideally use LED fairy lights as they are both more energy efficient and can be left on longer without danger of overheating.

Member's Method

My girlfriend and I like to reuse items and transform them into something that will suit our house. She has all these ideas for things that she can never find in the shops, so we adapt objects and materials to make them work! She came up with the idea for this headboard, using lengths of timber boards, with cushions hung from them.

We made it slightly differently at first, with just one plank of narrow wood. My girlfriend thought it looked wrong and said I'd put it too high up. She said she wanted more planks of wood and the cushions to be lowered. So I tracked down four pieces of 25cm-wide timber, nailed them to battens attached to the wall and made a bigger headboard. I stained the boards to give them a bit of colour.

My girlfriend made the cushions with hanging loops, and we hung them from coat hooks that I'd screwed into the boards above each side of the bed. The finishing touch was a string of fairy lights, which I draped behind the boards and looped around the coat hooks. She loved the end result!

Toni's Top Tip

You could achieve a similar effect by hanging cushions on loops from a curtain pole fixed above the bed.

Members' Comments

Beautiful – very rustic chic!! *Diana Shayler*

That is so different, unusual and brilliant. *Jill Tyson*

Absolutely stunning. Love it – it's so quirky. *Cara Parker*

Budget and Schedule Planner

Vision: What do you want to achieve?

Start with the end product so you have a clear idea of where you are going. Pictures, sketches and mood boards can help here, and you can refer back to them as you progress and/or use them for motivation.

My Vision

Budget

Once you've costed everything you need, start looking for savings wherever possible using the 7 Golden Rules on page 8, including borrowing, reusing, deal-hunting and hiring equipment.

Use the table below to work out your budget.

WHAT YOU NEED	Cost	GOLDEN RULE SAVING OPTION	Savings
	£		£
	£		£
	£		£
	£		£
	£		£
	£		£
	£		£
	£		£
	£		£
TOTAL COST £		TOTAL SAVINGS £	

Total cost – total savings = budget £

Overspend contingency of 10% £

Total £

Schedule

Breaking down your project into tasks and steps can help make larger projects more manageable and less daunting, and can give you a clear path to achieving your goal. If you're short on funds, you can also plan to get to a point where you can enjoy your progress to date while you save towards doing more.

TASKS/STEPS	TARGET COMPLETION DATE
1	
2	
3	
4	
5	
6	
7	
8	
9	
10	

Nooks and Crannies

Regardless of whether you live in a studio flat or a large detached house, every home has its fair share of those little spaces, tucked away in corners, under the stairs and within alcoves, that you look at and think, 'Why on earth did they build it like that, and what can I do with that wasted space?'

Rather than feel frustrated that you can't steal the space for another room, these nooks and crannies can offer an opportunity to provide you with vital storage space for awkward items, or can function as brand new mini rooms.

This section is full of ideas to transform these unloved corners into unique features or, perhaps, your new favourite place in your home. Somewhere to relax, get dressed or work? Maybe you just haven't considered it yet.

> **Understairs Cupboards**

How many of these words and phrases bring to mind your cupboard under the stairs? Messy, dusty, cluttered, muddy football boots, kitchen appliances that never get used (pasta-maker, anyone?) and, the most maddening of all, the carrier bag full of one hundred other carrier bags. If your cupboard is anywhere near organized, then one hundred gold stars for you. For everyone else, read on.

Given how an understairs cupboard is often small, narrow and cramped, it can be a challenging, cluttered space to get right. Out of sight, out of mind is how many of us think of this useful part of our home, which is why it often becomes a dumping ground. With some simple solutions, there's no reason why you can't turn it into an effective, tidy and aesthetically pleasing area.

1   Put up a shelf just below ceiling height – this dead space often gets ignored; however, it's a great place to store items you don't use every day but still need to be accessible.

2   A lot of people forget to do something with the back of the cupboard door – it's a whole wall just waiting to be used! Add some hooks and slimline baskets or trays/ shelves and you've created storage space where there was none. Magic!

3   The back of the door can also serve a dual purpose. If you don't have a suitable wall in your hallway for a full-length mirror, fix one to the back of the door so that you can check your outfit before you head out.

4 If you're working with a tight space or one with strange angles, cut some pieces of MDF that you can attach to the wall using wall brackets – to make affordable, custom-made shelves that fit your space and are perfect for storing shoes or spare cleaning supplies. You could also buy some plastic or wicker caddies, to double up on your options for organizing things and to keep everything tucked away neatly.

5 Use affordable modular storage to create handy homes for your items. Instead of chucking all your bits and pieces in the space together, if you have a full-length cupboard, the vacuum, mop and bucket, and the carrier-bag bag all have their place.

6 We're not suggesting you become the Dursleys and lock your children under the stairs, but this small space can work perfectly as a cosy chillout or reading zone. Use glow-in-the-dark decals and stickers with some coloured lighting to create a multi-sensory area that your kids can retreat to. If you like that idea too much, don't keep it for the kids – squeeze a single chair (or a bench with some cushions), some blankets and a wall-mounted lamp under the stairs and you have somewhere you can hide away for ten minutes to read a book, mess on your phone or just get some peace and quiet.

> **Recessed Shelves**

This is a great idea that can be used in any corner of your home. If it's a drywall construction, you can remove the plasterboard and use the space inside the walls as a shelving alcove.

ALLOW TIME FOR . . .

- **Glue, wood filler and paint to dry**

WHAT YOU NEED

- **Safety goggles**
- **Ear defenders**
- **Respirator mask**
- **Stud finder**
- **Pencil**
- **Spirit level**
- **Rafter square**
- **Utility knife**
- **Plasterboard saw**
- **Tape measure**
- **18mm-thick plywood (minimum) – for the back panel, four sides and shelves (see Toni's Top Tip on page 271)**
- **Wood glue**
- **Clamps**
- **Nails or screws (size to fit your shelf)**
- **Hammer or nail gun (if using nails)**
- **Screwdriver or screw gun (if using screws)**

- Mitre saw
- Wood trim (Scotia, beading or stripwood moulding, for example) – to fit around the recess as a decorative finish
- Decorator's caulk
- Wood filler
- Primer and paint

HOW TO

1   Get your safety gear on! A fair amount of dust and some splinters are going to be thrown into the air, and you don't want to get injured.

2   Use your stud finder to find the edges of your studs in relation to where you'd like to create your recessed shelves. If you don't have a stud finder, knock along the wall. Where the sound is dull rather than hollow is the likely position of a stud.

3   Using two studs as the outer edges of your intended recess, mark the area that you will be cutting out – use a spirit level and rafter square for accuracy, and leave space for a decorative moulding around the edge.

4   Use your utility knife to score along your markings, then cut inside this outline using your plasterboard saw (but be careful not to cut through to the plasterboard on the other side of the wall!).

5   Your cut should be perfectly flush with the studs – trim back as much excess plasterboard as is necessary to

achieve this. Double check your top and bottom cuts are level, and that your corners are perfect right angles.

6   It's now time to create the shelving area. First, measure he exact dimensions of the recess, including its height, width and depth. Cut a piece of plywood the same size as the recess's height and width to be the back 'wall' of your shelving area.

7   Next, take the height and the depth measurements of the hole but, crucially, subtract the thickness of the plywood from the original depth to account for the presence of your new back wall. Cut two pieces of plywood according to these measurements to create the sides of the shelving area.

8   Once you have the back and side pieces, use them as a guide to create top and bottom pieces, so that you can construct a frame that will sit within the recess, as well as however many shelves you want to add. Keep checking your pieces against the recess to ensure accuracy.

9   Use wood glue and clamps to hold the frame together, then use nails (with the help of a nail gun or a hammer) or screws (with the assistance of a screwdriver or a screw gun) to join the pieces together securely, before slotting in the shelves themselves and nailing/screwing them in place from outside of the frame. Leave the glue to dry according to manufacturer's instructions.

10 Position the frame inside the recess and secure it to the studs using nails or screws.

11 Once the shelves are in place, cover the rough edges of the recess outline using wood trim. To do this, use the mitre saw to cut the trim to fit the outline of your recess, ensuring it covers up the ragged plasterboard edges. Hold your pieces of trim up to the wall to make sure they're the right length before gluing them.

12 Once you're happy with the trim positioning, use wood glue to attach the pieces to the shelving frame, then nail them in place so the borders of the recess are completely covered. Again, leave the glue to dry.

13 Caulk the outside edge (where the trim meets the wall) and the interior seams, leave to dry following the manufacturer's instructions, then use wood filler to cover any nail holes or gaps. Leave to dry according to the manufacturer's instructions, then sand to smooth.

14 All that's left to do is to make it look pretty – apply a good few coats of primer to achieve an even finish, then apply the paint colour of your choice, ensuring you leave sufficient drying time between each coat.

Toni's Top Tip

Make sure you have enough plywood before you get started, by deciding on the size of your recess ahead of time. Measure the space you want to cut into, decide how many shelves you want to fit, and estimate the depth of the stud to allow for excess.

> Box Room

Two words that might spell dread for some but opportunity for others. Tiny box rooms might often seem pointless, but there's always more you can do to make yours work for you and your family. From clever decorative ideas that can transform a small space, to functional furniture ideas that will ensure no space goes to waste, read on for solutions to your box-room conundrum.

- If you want to keep the room as a bedroom, storage and space are key considerations. Don't buy a bed that's too big for the room, and go for one that has storage potential – either built-in drawers or space underneath where you can slip storage bags or boxes (see page 233).

- Make use of multi-functional furniture. Choose a bedside table that has drawers or an integrated cabinet, and fit floor-to-ceiling cupboards to maximize your storage options. This approach will help you to get the most out of your space by using areas that are often ignored while enabling you to keep your floor space uncluttered.

- Fitted wardrobes and shelves are another clever solution. Constructing them around your doorway can create a cosy opening that maximizes storage space, as can fitting shelves above the door frame.

- If your box room is too small to serve as a bedroom, why not use it as an office or a study? Add a simple desk, some lighting and some bookshelves. If the space is large enough, you could always add a sofa bed so that it can double up as a spare room when needed.

- Another solution for a too-small box room is a chillout room or a cosy snug in a busy household. It could be the perfect place for a small sofa, where you can curl up and read, or a TV to watch in peace, or even somewhere for the kids' games consoles so they have a separate space where they can play games with their friends.

> Decorating Your Small Space

Whether you've gone for a cosy corner or a tranquil retreat, here are a few tips on how to decorate the space:

- If you want to make any space appear bigger and brighter, your first port of call should be mirrors, and plenty of them. Opting for a number of well-placed wall mirrors will help make the room look bigger and will also reflect light within it, which in turn will make the room seem more light and airy.

- Your lighting choices are as, if not more, important than the mirrors. Good lighting will create an inviting sense of cosiness, so think about how lamps and wall lights can be arranged in a space to create a feeling of warmth.

- Go bold on the colours. It might seem counter-intuitive to go for a darker colour in a small room, but that's not necessarily the case. If you get your lighting right, a deep blue or olive green will result in a calming chic vibe. The trick is to pick the right shade for your space and light it well so that it doesn't feel gloomy.

- Alternatively, go light and bright with your colour scheme. Light and neutral tones will create a natural sense of serenity.

- Make decisive choices with your decor. Small rooms can make a single decorative item look a lot more striking than it would in a larger room, whereas putting lots of items on the walls or ornaments on the shelves can make the space feel crowded. Be sparing with your decoration to give the room more focus and ensure it doesn't feel cluttered.

> Mini Office Space

For years, most of us dreamed of working from home, then the Covid pandemic made that a reality for many, whether they wanted it or not! Dining-room and kitchen tables were transformed from places to eat to makeshift workspaces for adults, who were often simultaneously home-schooling children by their side. Some were resigned to perching on the edge of their beds with laptops propped up on ironing boards.

With working from home, in one form or another, looking like it's going to stay for a while, setting up a home-working or studying space is a sensible thing to do. Not everyone has a spare room where they can set up a home office, so, with budget and space in mind, here are some creative ideas to make your working day go smoothly, even with a house full of people.

- The bedroom is many people's first choice for a home office, but the danger comes at night when you can't properly shut off from work and go to sleep. So why not convert part of your living room into a working space instead? You could put a small, narrow desk in a corner of your living room, or repurpose a sideboard or wall-mounted unit as your worktop. The benefit of using a wall-mounted unit as your makeshift desk is that it enables you to have a standing desk, which is good for your health and productivity. If you prefer to sit, then ensure your chair can fit under the wall-mounted unit, enabling you to sit comfortably while working.

- If you're feeling practical, you could build your own desk to fit a space of your choosing – even a piece of wood that's 60cm wide can accommodate a laptop if you only need a small surface for occasional use.

- Try hanging a room-dividing curtain or screen to separate your office from the rest of the room. If you're working in the living room, you could install a desk in a fitted floor-to-ceiling cupboard so that you can close the doors on your work at the end of the day and turn the room back into a relaxing space.

- Fit some simple wooden boards onto shelf brackets and fix them to an unused wall at chest height in your kitchen, living room or a spare room. Use this as a standing desk or couple it with a high stool to create a seated workstation. The standing-desk option not only takes up much less floor space, it's good for you, as mentioned above.

- Transform a nook. Some rooms have natural alcoves owing to structural features of the property – perhaps either side of an old chimney breast or by a window. You could use this useless space and install a wall-mounted desk across the expanse. Cut some wood to size, either by hand or at your local DIY store, and mount it on simple brackets. When not in use, this could double up as a handy shelf.

- Try a fold-away desk, which will allow you to create an office space for the day. At night, you can fully put it away.

- We often see our hallway merely as the route from one room to another, but fitting a narrow desk or floating shelf on a landing or in a downstairs hallway might prove a useful use of space you hadn't considered before. The desk could then double up as a console table for you or your kids when the work or school day is done.

- The kitchen table is the go-to workspace for many, but have you considered a breakfast bar instead? Pair with some high stools and you have a multi-functional desk that will also have a life outside working hours (see page 129).

- Converting your kitchen counter will work only if you have adequate space to sit properly at it, but countertops can create great temporary desk spaces where you can set up your office during the day. Buy a tray to pack away your workspace easily in the evening when it's time for dinner! Plus, your office is now right by the fridge . . .

> Kids' Play Area

Creating a space where children can learn, grow and have fun in their early years is so important for their development and wellbeing, as well as giving you some peace and quiet while they're ensconced in their space. The idea of pulling off some kind of elaborate kids' wonderland may be something of a stretch, but there are myriad budget-friendly ways to put together a multi-functional space your children will love as they get older. If you don't have the luxury of a dedicated room to convert into a kids' play area, you can still carve out a corner of their bedroom or the kitchen/diner for this purpose. Here are some of the best dos and don'ts to keep in mind when creating an awesome kids' play area, from decor to DIY.

Do . . .

Choose a hardwearing washable paint. Kids make a mess – it's a universal fact. Opting for a durable washable paint means you can simply wipe away marks, smudges and handprints. Think about your finish, too – eggshell on woodwork shows up fingerprints a lot less than gloss.

Go for a theme. There are so many ways to get creative without tying yourself into the decorating side of things and overspending. Pick up some fake vines and foliage that you can attach to the ceiling and walls to create a jungle theme. Create a pirate's lair with fancy-dress costumes and nautical props. Peelable stickers of planets and stars cost next to nothing, and, paired with some colour LED light strips, will help you create an amazing intergalactic space station for your little ones.

Consider an accent wall. Pick a fun wallpaper for one wall, or perhaps choose an area to cover with chalkboard paint (see page 182). Whether it's a whole wall or just a large section, when the kids tell you they've drawn on the wall, it won't be a problem.

Go second-hand. Upcycle, repurpose and adapt. Older bits of furniture can be turned into pieces perfect for the playroom. Have fun decorating these items with the kids – let them choose a colour or get them to splash the surfaces with paint. You'll end up with a set of multi-coloured art-tastic drawers they'll love. The joy of doing this with them is that the furniture can be adapted to fit their needs and style as they grow up, and they'll learn some useful skills along the way.

Create a children's art gallery. Asking your kids to create their own works of art for the walls gives them the chance to show off their masterpieces and costs you nothing. Hang a length of string from one wall to another (ideally out of their reach), and use pegs to attach their artwork to it.

Build your own storage. A perfect way to save some money is to build some storage bins out of MDF, screws and wood glue (making sure you sand down any rough edges and add rubber corners to prevent accidental bumps and grazes). The beauty of this idea is that you can create storage that matches your space but costs very little, and if (when!) it gets knocked about by the kids, no problem.

Don't . . .

Decorate just for the age your kids are now. They grow up fast and their tastes change, so decorate in neutral tones that can be updated over time. Use accent colours for your accessories and go for budget-friendly decorations that can be easily upgraded.

Neglect storage. This is probably the most important thing to consider. As kids grow, they accumulate more toys, so unless you're going to regularly negotiate getting rid of these, you're going to need as much storage as you can manage. Pick up a range of affordable storage bins in different sizes, for smaller and larger toys. A storage ottoman gives them somewhere to sit and another place to keep their stuff.

Forget the walls. Your storage solutions don't just have to sit on the floor. Hang fabric pouches and colourful hooks from the walls and backs of doors for vertical options.

Overlook soft furnishings. Bean bags, cushions and blankets can all be picked up from supermarkets or bargain stores for next to nothing. They provide the perfect materials for building dens as well as offering somewhere comfortable for the kids to sit while they're playing.

Forget about the floor. If the floor in your kids' play area is hard, put down something to make it more comfortable. Choose a washable rug to add some much-needed cushioning against falls, and to help keep things clean. The cheaper the rug, the less you'll be bothered when there's an inevitable spillage.

Think decor just means paint. Stickers, decals and posters are all fantastic options. You can pick these up for pennies, and easily change them.

Kids' Play Area

Toni's Choice

Using a nook or a cranny to magically create a kids' play area from an otherwise unused space is a speciality of the DIY OAB group. We all know space is at a premium in a busy household, but that children love having their own space, if you can possibly create one for them. I've chosen Jade Simpson's project as a brilliant way of giving her son a den of his own by building one in the space above their staircase: forget a cupboard beneath the stairs, this is a cool den above them! This is quite a complex build, though, and you'll note that Jade employed a joiner, so do enlist help with professionals if any of this seems beyond your current skillset. Depending on whether you plaster or not, you'll need to allow the plaster to dry before you paint, and as you know by now, you always need to allow time for each coat of paint to dry.

WHAT YOU NEED

- Mallet and/or plasterboard saw
- Timber struts
- Screws
- Power drill
- 18mm-thick plywood
- Protective gloves and goggles
- Plasterboard
- Mitre saw
- Plaster and associated tools including a bucket for mixing, a hand board, bucket trowel and plastering trowel for application
- Paint
- Roller and paint brush
- Roller tray
- Carpet offcut
- Desk lamp
- Children's ladder from online exchange or a charity shop

HOW TO

1 Knock through the wall above your staircase to access the available space there using a mallet and/or plasterboard saw.

2 Build struts in the floor and walls, secured to the walls using screws, ensuring that the floor struts are sound and weight bearing.

3   Wearing your gloves and goggles, measure and cut plasterboard sheets for the space. Screw these to the struts using your power drill.

4   Plaster the plasterboard if you're up for the challenge – it's a complicated and skilled process, though, so check an online tutorial before you think of doing this, or draft in some help from a professional plasterer. Alternatively, skip this step and simply paint the plasterboard.

5   Paint the plasterboard, using appropriate paint – consult your DIY shop when buying the plasterboard. If you haven't applied plaster, then apply a layer of PVA primer first and allow to dry. Then paint with PVA paint suitable for use on PVA primer to ensure the paint adheres.

6   Lay plywood over the floor and screw this into the floor struts.

7   Use a carpet offcut from another room to carpet the floor space.

8   Add a desk lamp to create a cosy atmosphere, or stick some LED light strips in the space.

9   Screw the ladder into the floor struts to ensure that it's safe and secure.

Member's Method

After moving into our project house last year, we noticed that in the hallway at the top of the stairs, there was a lot of unused space next to our son's bedroom. We decided to make a raised den for him there, by breaking through his wall and using the void above the stairs.

With the help of our joiner, who was working on the house at the time, we built a frame for the space using timber struts, then screwed this into the brickwork and studwork of his opened-up wall. We then plasterboarded inside and outside the frame and plastered it.

We made a floor for the den using plywood, then used an old piece of carpet so that things were softer underfoot. We got some free ladders from Facebook Marketplace and put them in place for him to access the space.

Our son loves it up there – it's his own safe place to game. His friends all love it too.

Watch Out!

If you install or include lights in kids' dens, you'll need to be extra vigilant about switching them off when not in use. Ideally only install LED lights, which are energy efficient and do not give off heat.

Only design a den involving a ladder for older children, to avoid accidents.

Members' Top Tips

- LED light strips are a fun and easy way to add lighting to a kids' den. These lights also put the child in charge of their lighting scheme, as the strips often come with a remote control to change the colour of the lights!

Members' Comments

Looks amazing!!! Love it *Mindy Mann*

Looks amazing – you are very clever and talented xx
Karen Fantarrow Darby

Wow, that's awesome! *Karen Minikin*

Budget and Schedule Planner

Vision: What do you want to achieve?

Start with the end product so you have a clear idea of where you are going. Pictures, sketches and mood boards can help here, and you can refer back to them as you progress and/or use them for motivation.

My Vision

Budget

Once you've costed everything you need, start looking for savings wherever possible using the 7 Golden Rules on page 8, including borrowing, reusing, deal-hunting and hiring equipment.

Use the table below to work out your budget.

WHAT YOU NEED	Cost	GOLDEN RULE SAVING OPTION	Savings
	£		£
	£		£
	£		£
	£		£
	£		£
	£		£
	£		£
	£		£
	£		£
TOTAL COST £		TOTAL SAVINGS £	

Total cost – total savings = budget £

Overspend contingency of 10% £

Total £

Schedule

Breaking down your project into tasks and steps can help make larger projects more manageable and less daunting, and can give you a clear path to achieving your goal. If you're short on funds, you can also plan to get to a point where you can enjoy your progress to date while you save towards doing more.

TASKS/STEPS	TARGET COMPLETION DATE
1	
2	
3	
4	
5	
6	
7	
8	
9	
10	

Acknowledgements

First and foremost, I couldn't finish this book without thanking the incredible DIY OAB community. Without the creativity, inventiveness and passion of our members, none of this would be possible – so thank you all, from the bottom of my heart.

I'd especially like to thank my wonderful children, Kayleigh, Harrison and Freddie, who are infinitely patient with my never-ending DIY projects, and who give me the confidence and the motivation to keep pushing myself, even when the dreaded imposter syndrome kicks in.

I'm also eternally grateful to my brilliant agent, Clare Hulton, and to the team at Transworld who have brought this book to life.

Thank you to Lee Wilcox, Adam Barrie, Andy Taylor, Mark Collins and Ian Collins for believing in DIY OAB, and to everyone at Electric House. I would also like to thank George Gabriel for his ongoing support.

For their help in compiling the book, I'd like to thank Beth Blance, George Smith, Madeline Charles, Simon Fooks, Andy Wilcox and Helena Caldon. For the jacket design, Beci Kelly and Tony Maddock; for the book design, Bobby Birchall; and for the illustrations, May van Millingen. For their help in moderating the DIY OAB group, I'd like to thank Chantelle Shemmans, Cheryl Rozee, Jessamy Eloise Sprague and Toni Rees, and for helping me with everything, Katie Pearson and Carol Lovegrove.

Finally, I want to thank you for picking up and reading this book. Everyone should be able to create a home they love, and by becoming a part of the DIY OAB movement, you're helping to make that vision a reality.

Good luck, keep creating, and remember to share your DIY adventures with the DIY OAB family!